THE
BRISTOL CITY
MISCELLANY

For my son, Harry Ethan

THE
BRISTOL CITY
MISCELLANY

DAVID CLAYTON

First published 2009
This new edition in paperback first published in 2012

The History Press
The Mill, Brimscombe Port
Stroud, Gloucestershire, GL5 2QG
www.thehistorypress.co.uk

British Library Cataloguing in Publication Data.
A catalogue record for this book is available from the British
Library.

ISBN 978 0 7524 8628 4

Typesetting and origination by The History Press
Printed in Great Britain
Manufacturing managed by Jellyfish Print Solutions Ltd

Foreword

by Shaun Goater

I loved my time at Ashton Gate and will always have a place in my heart for Bristol City and their supporters. When my wife Anita and I came to look around the city in the summer of 1996, we thought it was the closest place to Bermuda we'd come across since leaving our home island almost a decade earlier. The sun was shining, I could smell the sea and there were seagulls everywhere – heaven after seven years under the leaden skies of Rotherham!

The City fans were quick to get behind me and I'd like to think I repaid that faith out on the pitch. Many games stick in my mind but the hat-tricks against Notts County and Wigan evoke particularly strong memories for me.

We were gunning for the title in 1997/98 when I was sold to Manchester City – it was a massive move for me, even though they were on their way to relegation from Division One – but ultimately, it gave me a chance of playing in the Premiership. I'd always dreamed at playing at the highest level in England and even though I was extremely happy in Bristol, I couldn't turn down the chance of fast-tracking my ambition. If I'd been worried about the reaction of the people of Bristol to that move, I shouldn't have been because the reception I got when I finally returned to Ashton Gate will stay with me forever. It must have been scripted that my final game before retirement would be for Southend, my final club, away to Bristol City. With the Southend, Bristol City and several hundred Manchester City fans all singing 'Feed the Goat', it's a day I'll never forget.

I was delighted to be asked to write the first few words of this book and I hope you enjoy *The Bristol City Miscellany* as much as I have – maybe there'll be one or two facts about the club you didn't know. Test me if you see me next time I'm in town! Feed the Goat – with facts!

Shaun 'Lenny' Goater, Bermuda, 2009

Introduction & Acknowledgements

I loved the old Ashton Gate with its mixture of terracing, paddocks and dilapidated stands, and I'll miss it sorely when City move to their new state-of-the-art home in the not-too-distant future. Kevin Mabbutt and Gerry Gow have always been my favourite players. This is a club that deserves Premier League football and I reckon we'll have exactly that by the time they lock Ashton Gate up for the last time. Well, we can dream, can't we?

I hope you enjoy reading this book as much as I enjoyed writing it and if you do, buy me a cider and then down it for me – I'll be with you in spirit. Briefly, thanks to Michelle Tilling, my editor at The History Press and thanks to my wife and three young children, Harry, Jaime and Chrissie. That's pretty much it for this one as most of the digging was done by Yours Truly – for facts and figures from elsewhere, the City stats pages proved invaluable as were the books by Peter Godsiff, Ivan Ponting and Tom Morgan – thanks to all of them.

David Clayton, 2012

'This club could be the Manchester United of the West Country. The opportunity is there and all we have to do is seize it. The potential fan base is colossal, but we've got to give the people something they can really believe in. There is a special aura about this place, so much has happened here down the years – and it's dripping with a magic that is still untapped.'

John Atyeo (1932–93)

GARY JOHNSONISMS

'I am a Championship manager, but you mustn't
treat it like the actual computer game, *Championship
Manager*.'

Gary Johnson – PC as ever

'Lee's been a great player for us and we have to see that.
On occasions, he may not be the best player on the
pitch, but we need him around.'

Johnno on his son, Lee

'We couldn't have been drawn against a higher-placed
team, as they are currently second to Everton.'

Johnno confounds the laws of mathematics

'I might be pleased with the point on Sunday, but at the
moment I'm not. I felt we had enough decent chances
and I'm still fuming about the one that wasn't.'

**Johnno reacts in riddles to a goal that never was at
Sheffield Wednesday**

'Yes, more than one or two were ill. We took them
to a place where maybe they hadn't been. That was
important to me. I wanted them to know they had a bit
more in the tank, even if they felt ill. There'll be no extra
day off. They do deserve it – but they ain't going to get
it! The good thing is they'll be working with a smile on
their face.'

**Johnno – hard taskmaster and fitness guru ups the levels
of training after a disappointing loss**

'If Fontaine scores I'll bare my behind in Burtons window.'

Johnno, banking on the thought of such horrors inspiring goals for shot-shy striker Liam Fontaine – it did!

'I don't usually speak to anyone over 30, never mind sign them.'

Gary Johnson – promoting ageism?

THE GAFFERS

Bob Hewison's seventeen-year reign as boss took in the Second World War years and an eight-month suspension, but he remains easily in pole position, with Alan Dicks the second longest-serving boss on thirteen years. Alex Raisbeck and Pat Beasley (both eight years) and Sam Hollis, who also spent eight years in charge – though over three different periods – are also worthy of note. Roy Hodgson (four months), Tony Pulis (six months), Benny Lennartsson, Denis Smith (ten months) and the ill-fated partnership of Tony Fawthorp and David Burnside (five months) all spent less than a year in the hot seat. The full list is:

Manager	From	To
Sam Hollis	April 1897	April 1899
Robert Campbell	May 1899	June 1901
Sam Hollis	June 1901	April 1905
Harry Thickett	May 1905	October 1910
Frank Bacon	October 1910	January 1911
Sam Hollis	January 1911	April 1913
George Hedley	April 1913	January 1917

Jack Hamilton	January 1917	May 1919
Joe Palmer	May 1919	October 1921
Alex Raisbeck	December 1921	July 1929
Joe Bradshaw	August 1929	February 1932
Bob Hewison	April 1932	March 1949*
Bob Wright	April 1949	June 1950
Pat Beasley	July 1950	January 1958
Peter Doherty	January 1958	March 1960
Fred Ford	July 1960	September 1967
Alan Dicks	October 1967	September 1980
Bobby Houghton	October 1980	January 1982
Roy Hodgson	January 1982	April 1982
Terry Cooper	May 1982	March 1988
Joe Jordan	March 1988	September 1990
Jimmy Lumsden	September 1990	February 1992
Denis Smith	March 1992	January 1993
Russell Osman	January 1993	November 1994
Joe Jordan	November 1994	March 1997
John Ward	March 1997	October 1998
Benny Lennartsson	October 1998	July 1999
Tony Pulis	July 1999	January 2000
Tony Fawthorp/ David Burnside	January 2000	May 2000
Danny Wilson	June 2000	July 2004
Brian Tinnion	July 2004	September 2005
Gary Johnson	September 2005	March 2010
Steve Coppell	April 2010	August 2010
Keith Millen	August 2010	October 2011
Derek McInnes	October 2011	present

* Bob Hewison was suspended between October 1938 and May 1939 – club skipper Clarrie Burton took on player/manager duties during the intervening period.

BASIL, BALDRICK & BUTTONS

Weston-super-Mare-born John Cleese, creator of the finest British sitcom ever – *Fawlty Towers* – is perhaps City's most famous supporter, though there is an impressive list of celebrities after his name. Baldrick himself – Tony Robinson, of *Time Team* and *Blackadder* fame and F1 racing driver Jenson Button follow the Robins, as does *Sunday Night Project* host Justin Lee Collins. Deputy Editor of the *Sun*, Dominic Mohan, plus graffiti artist Banksy and former England cricketer Marcus Trescothick have all professed their love for City at some point and former Bath and England rugby union star Gareth Chilcott is not an uncommon face at Ashton Gate. Add BBC commentator Jonathan Pearce, comedians Russell Howard and Mark Watson and there's only Somerset's finest, The Wurzels, missing!

RELEGATION FARCE

It all came down the last day of the 1976/77 season. City had fought so hard to get into the top division and they weren't going to go down without a battle. One of three teams – Coventry City, Sunderland and the Robins – would join Tottenham and Stoke City in Division Two and, as fixture lists often do, the irony was City were away to Coventry on the final day. There were numerous permutations and Sunderland had the best goal difference, but the fact was if City drew, their safety would be guaranteed. More than 15,000 Bristolians made their way to Highfield Road for the showdown and after just 15 minutes, they were biting their nails anxiously as Tommy Hutchison put the Sky Blues ahead. In a tense affair, relegation looked a certainty when Hutchison made it 2–0 after 52 minutes, but it took the Robins just 90 seconds to begin their fightback. Gerry Gow reduced arrears on 54 minutes and 11 minutes from time the City fans went wild as Donnie Gillies equalised from 10 yards. Suddenly it was Coventry who looked like going down, particularly if Sunderland were level or winning away to Everton.

With 4 minutes remaining and on the instructions of Coventry managing director and *Match of the Day* anchorman Jimmy Hill, the scoreboard then flashed up a latest score: Everton 2 Sunderland 0. Both sets of fans began celebrating – except if a winning goal went in for either City or Coventry, the loser would still be relegated. The solution was simple – play out time and make sure both teams survived. What had been a blood and thunder contest suddenly became a stroll in the park with City keeping the ball in their own half for the last 5 minutes, unchallenged by Coventry. Eventually a bemused referee blew for full-time and the celebrations began in earnest. Thank goodness for Jimmy Hill . . . not many times you'd say that in a lifetime!

FA YOUTH CUP

City have only ever reached the final of England's most prestigious youth competition – the FA Youth Cup – on one occasion. In 1973 City's talented teens faced Bobby Robson's Ipswich Town in a two-legged final, with Ipswich taking what proved to be an unassailable 3–0 first-leg lead at Portman Road. The mountain proved too great to climb for the young City side and despite a gallant 1–1 draw at Ashton Gate, City lost 4–1 on aggregate to, it has to be said, an exceptionally talented Ipswich side who were to win the competition again just two years later.

NICKNAMES

There have been several memorable nicknames for City players over the years, some funny, some a little on the insulting side! Case in point, one of City's greatest players, Billy Wedlock was nicknamed 'Fatty' because of his sturdy build – Wedlock, as with everything else in life, took it all in his stride and accepted it was an affectionate tag rather than anything more sinister. Paul 'Ago' Agostino was a little less original and Wayne 'Chief' Allison was questionable to say the least. Dariusz 'Jacki' Dziekanowski was for practical reasons, while Shaun Goater became universally known as 'the Goat' after he left Ashton Gate. He had been nicknamed 'Lenny' because his first name is actually Leonard.

BATH TIME

After Rovers, Bath City is the closest club to Ashton Gate. Surprisingly, the clubs have met just three times (excluding friendlies) with the Robins winning two and drawing the other.

CLUB LEGEND: JOHN ATYEO

At most football clubs, supporters will argue into the night about who their team's greatest player was – at Bristol City, there is no argument – it IS John Atyeo. Born Peter John Walter Atyeo on 7 February 1932, he was nineteen when city chairman Harry Dolman drove to railway signalman Walter Atyeo's home in Dilton Marsh, Wiltshire. Walter's son John was making quite an impression and the teenage forward had already played twice for First Division champions Portsmouth in the previous campaign – but only as an amateur. With Pompey desperate to sign up Atyeo, Dolman thought he'd steal a march on them by making a personal visit to meet the youngster, but was aghast when he arrived to find the Bristol Rovers manager Bert Tann's car parked near to the Atyeo home. He bided his time and waited for Tann to leave before making his move and, after several hours of negotiation, a personal contract was agreed between chairman and player – it was an amazing coup for City and if anyone doubted the youngster's potential, his debut against Newport County in which he made two goals and scored another quickly convinced them otherwise!

Atyeo quickly became a terrace idol, but he was only playing for the club on a part-time basis while he continued his apprenticeship as a quantity surveyor. He eventually doubled his training schedule from two to four days, but he remained steadfast in his attitude that football wasn't the be all and end all in his life. Still, the plaudits poured down on his sturdy shoulders and in January 1955, he won successive England Under-23 caps against Italy and Scotland, scoring in each game. He would eventually win five full caps for England, scoring six goals in the process and partnered Stanley Matthews, but despite helping his country reach the 1958 World Cup finals, he was omitted from the squad with the selectors unconvinced by his part-time status and the fact he was playing for a club outside the top division. Of course, Atyeo could have held his own against the best in the world and he should have gone on to become an England legend, but it wasn't to be and the national team's loss was City's gain. He went on to be the top goal-scorer for twelve of the fifteen seasons he graced Ashton Gate and never played professionally in the top division.

A prolific scorer, when he finally hung up his boots to move into teaching, he'd played 647 times for the Robins and scored an incredible 351 goals – a record that will surely never be surpassed. Coveted by the best teams in the world, he spurned the opportunity to play for AC Milan, Liverpool, Chelsea and Tottenham Hotspur to remain with City and when a new stand was mooted to replace the Park End, by public demand it was decided to name it the Atyeo Stand.

Tragically, just a few weeks before its completion, Atyeo died suddenly at the age of sixty-one. John Atyeo loved the simple life, was humble and something of a gentle giant – he was never booked in his career, despite taking some fearful punishment by those of lesser ability. City plan to build a statue in the great man's honour at the club's new stadium – a fitting tribute to a player whose personal achievements are unlikely to ever be surpassed.

BY GEORGE – WE'VE SCORED!

Nobody likes a 'homer' referee, but in 1895, Bristol South End – soon to become Bristol City – had somehow attracted the mighty Preston North End to the city to play what was no more than a newly-formed amateur team – it was an incredible coup by the ambitious committee behind Bristol South End but Preston only agreed if there was a guaranteed £40 fee paid. On 6 April, South End and North End took to the field amid a torrential downpour that kept thousands of people away. Though, as expected, Preston won comfortably, perhaps the referee encapsulated the excitement of the people of Bristol when South End scored what was clearly an illegal goal following a charge into the Preston goalkeeper by Hammer Clements. Referee George Elmes, instead of blowing for a foul, punched the air in delight and ran back to the centre circle shouting, 'Goal! Goal!' The reason? Elmes was Bristol South End's Vice-Chairman! Go on lad!

RAM RAIDERS

Three defeats and three draws was not the most inauspicious start to the 1923/24 season, but City fans could see their team seemed to be improving with each game. A trip to the Baseball Ground to take on Derby County for match number seven provided even more reason for the Robins supporters to believe their team would slowly start to climb the table after a thrilling 3–2 over the Rams. As was the way back in those days, City and Derby then met the following weekend and there was plenty of optimism among the Ashton Gate faithful that a quickfire league double would be completed . . . how wrong they were! Derby romped home 8–0 to register what was, and still is, City's record home defeat. After that sound thrashing, City's defence improved and conceded a single goal in each of their next four games and the team clearly were capable of better things. They held eventual champions Leeds United 0–0 at Elland Road and thrashed runners-up Bury 4–1 at Ashton Gate. Considering Derby finished third and the Robins also held fourth-placed Blackpool and fifth-placed Southampton to draws too, it was something of a mystery that City finished bottom of the table and were relegated.

ROYLE APPROVAL

Perhaps the most scintillating debut in City's history came when Joe Royle made his debut against Middlesbrough on 26 November 1977. Royle had become disillusioned with life at Manchester City where he was no longer guaranteed a first-team place and when he was offered a loan spell at Ashton Gate, he reluctantly accepted and went straight into the side to face Boro. Royle would get just four chances to score in his first game for the Robins – and he managed to tuck all four away! His first was a trademark header and he completed the perfect hat-trick by then adding one with his left and two more with his right in a 4–1 victory. Royle made the move permanent a few weeks later – by public demand – but failed to score again for City for the next ten games!

ANGLO-SCOTTISH CUP

City won their second recognised trophy in 1977 when they went all the way to the final of the Anglo-Scottish Cup and beat a team managed by then plain old Alex Ferguson. Typically, City began the path to the final with a defeat, losing 1–0 to Birmingham City, but victories over Bristol Rovers and Plymouth meant Alan Dicks' side progressed through to the last eight where Partick Thistle awaited. City lost the first leg 2–0 and it seemed the adventure was over, but two goals from Mann and another from Whitehead turned the tie on its head and City won 3–0 on the day and 3–2 on aggregate. Next up were Hibernian and the first leg of the semi-final was a stormy, bad-tempered affair that saw Norman Hunter sent off in the 73rd minute and City were reduced to nine men when Cormack gave Des Bremner an 'Edinburgh Kiss' (head-butt) four minutes later. Hibs missed a late penalty as City hung on for a creditable 1–1 draw. Afterwards, a disgusted Hibs chairman, Tom Hart, claimed he had no intention of letting his team take part in the second leg and dubbed the Robins 'The Butchers of Bristol'! Okay, Gerry Gow and Norman Hunter were a little, shall we say, enthusiastic, but butchers? Never. If in doubt, threaten a Scotsman in the pocket and after City demanded £12,000 compensation for Hibs' refusal to play, Hart relented and his team played – and lost – a thrilling second leg, played in torrential rain at Ashton Gate and won by 5–3 by City. The final, again to be played over two legs, pitted the Robins against rookie manager Alex Ferguson's St Mirren with the first leg played at Love Street. Goals from Kevin Mabbutt and Cormack seemed to be steering City towards the trophy, but Abercrombie pulled one back for St Mirren three minutes from time, giving Ferguson's side hope for the return match. On 5 December 1977, a crowd of 16,110 turned out at Ashton Gate for what they assumed would be a comfortable victory followed by the presentation of the Anglo-Scottish Cup, but St Mirren picked up where they'd left off in the previous game by levelling the aggregate score through Bobby Reid in the 68th minute. Mabbutt equalised within two minutes but the match looked destined to move into extra time when Frank McGarvey bundled home what appeared to be a perfectly legitimate second goal for the visitors a few moments from time. Referee Derek Nippard decided otherwise and gave a foul for McGarvey's challenge on Shaw and City clung on to win the cup 3–2 on aggregate. Alex Ferguson gave the officials the hairdryer treatment after the match and found himself in trouble with the authorities as a result – and not much has changed 30-odd years on!

ZENITH SYSTEMS CUP

City only appeared in the Zenith Data Systems Cup on two occasions, winning neither game. On the first occasion City played Oxford United at the Manor Ground in November 1990. After the game ended 2–2 following extra time, City lost 3–2 on penalties and exited stage left at the first hurdle. The following season and the Robins again went out at their first appearance, this time entering at the second round stage and losing 2–1 to Southampton in front of 5,782 Ashton Gate fans.

BERMUDAN SHORT

The beautiful British colonial island of Bermuda has a strong link with City, thanks entirely to former Ashton Gate hero Shaun Goater. 'The Goat' was honoured with his own tribute day on 21 June 2000 – officially named 'Shaun Goater Day'. Thousands turned out to watch his motorcade drive through the capital's streets. It's not an annual event, but is now famous in its own right and perhaps should be a yearly event – imagine the City fans that would flock over to pay homage to the Goat in such a beautiful setting!

A THEME IS BORN

On 18 September 1967 history was made at Ashton Gate. Halfway through a 3–1 tonking of Hull City the crowd began to sing 'Drink up thy cider' – the footballing debut of the scrumpy 'n' western musical genre. The song remains a favourite today. The Wurzels even made a record for City – the enigmatically titled 'One for the Bristol City'. This was a rewrite of The Wurzels' 'Morning Glory', and adopted by City as their theme song.

THE OTHER ROBINS

City's rivalry with Swindon Town – the other team also known as 'The Robins' – stretches back more than a century. The next time the two sides are in the same division will see the 99th and 100th meetings between the clubs – unless there are any cup meetings before then. City have the edge after 98 clashes between the teams with 42 wins, 30 draws and just 26 defeats to date.

Total record – City v Swindon:

Pld 98   W 42   D 30   L 26   F 157   A 121

SONGS

He's big,
he's fast,
his first name should be last,
Stern John, Stern John!

City fans serenade Watford's Carribean striker

Flying high up in the sky,
We'll keep the red flag flying high,
Cider heads until we die
We'll keep the red flag flying high.

Flying high up in the sky,
We'll keep the red flag flying high,
Cider heads until we die
We'll keep the red flag flying high.

An Ashton Gate favourite . . .

E I E I E I O,
Up the Football League we go,
When we get promotion,
This is what we will sing,
We are City,
We are City,
Johnson is our king . . .

A royal salute to Johnno

Drink up thee Cider, drink up thee Cider,
For tonight we'll merry be,
We're going down the Rovers to turn 'em over,
There's still more Cider in the jar.

Definitely a glass-half-full song

1 2 3 4 5
If you wanna stay alive (keep off the East end)
6 7 8 9 10
If you wanna walk again (keep off the East end)
East east East enders
East east East enders!

**And not a mention anywhere of Dot Cotton or the
Queen Vic!**

THE CURSE OF CLOUGHIE

Though not alone in this category, the Robins fared very
badly against Brian Clough's teams over the years. 'Old
Big 'Ead' began his managerial career at Hartlepool
United, though City never played them during that
period. The first meeting between a Clough team and
City proved to be the Robins' one and only success – a
1–0 win over Derby County during the 1967/68 season.
The return match at the Baseball Ground ended in a
3–1 defeat. The season after that, the Rams drew 0–0 at
Ashton Gate before winning the return 5–0 on the final
day of the campaign – the day Derby were crowned as
champions of Division Two. It was seven years before
City again took on Clough, by now Nottingham Forest's
manager. Still in Division Two in 1975/76, Forest won
both League games that year, triumphing 1–0 in Bristol

and 2–0 at the City Ground. The duel between City and Forest resumed in the top flight after both teams won promotion in succeeding years but while the division was different, the outcome was the same with Forest completing the double 1–0 at home and 3–1 at Ashton Gate on their way to the Division One title for the first time. The following season Forest again completed a League double, winning 3–1 at City and 2–0 in Nottingham. Whatever Clough was telling his troops when they played the Robins, it was working because a year later his talented team drew 1–1 in a League Cup fourth-round tie at Ashton Gate before winning the replay 3–0. Though City would never again face Forest in the League during Cloughie's era, they added a 2–1 FA Cup fifth-round victory in 1981 (at Forest) and, heartbreakingly, City's dreams of League Cup glory were ended by Clough's side at the semi-final stage in 1989 when City lost the home leg 1–0 before valiantly battling for a 1–1 draw in the return game, losing 2–1 on aggregate. The final locking of horns with arguably one of the best English managers of all time (who would retire a year later), was in 1992, when Forest denied City a place in the last eight of the FA Cup with a 4–1 drubbing at the City Ground.

Total record – City v Clough:

Pld 16	W 1	D 3	L 12	F 8	A 32

EARLY TO BED

Bedminster were the main rivals of Bristol South End and were never the friendliest of neighbours until the clubs officially merged in 1900. Prior to that, games between the teams were fiercely contested affairs, with only one of six games ending in a City win. The Robins' only win was a 2–1 victory, while Bedminster recorded a 6–0 victory on one occasion, one of three wins before the merger. Considering Ashton Gate was originally Bedminster's home ground, no true City fan would begrudge them those few wins.

CHRISTMAS CRACKERS

Yes, long before Arsène Wenger was moaning about having a month-long break over the festive period, the English programme regularly included a League fixture on Christmas Day. It's hard to believe the authorities would even consider a match on this most sacred of days, but on no fewer than thirty-one occasions, Bristol City took to the field on 25 December. The first two Christmases involved Barnsley, with the first game, in 1901, a 2–2 draw, staged in South Yorkshire and watched by around 3,000 shivering Tykes fans.

A year later and Barnsley travelled to Bristol where approximately 6,000 fans saw a thrilling 3–3 draw. In 1903, apparently the people of Bristol demanded they be saved of turkey and inane parlour games – well, 7,000 of them did anyway – and Bristol's only two professional clubs met for a Christmas Day cracker at Ashton Gate, with City winning 5–3.

The festive thriller was a fairly regular fixture on the League programme up until the mid-1950s when sense finally prevailed. It's worth noting, however, that the games were, more often than not, fairly well attended and City only lost one game out of seven Christmas Day fixtures after the Second World War. Did the people of Bristol support these games? Well a combined attendance of more than 53,000 for the last three 25 December games at Ashton Gate suggest they did.

City's complete Christmas Day record is:

Pld 31   W 12   D 12   L 7   F 57   A 56

THEY SAID IT…

'It's the greatest moment of my life!'

Alan Dicks celebrates promotion by addressing thousands of City fans at the end of the 1975/76 season

'Billy Wedlock was the finest gentleman I have ever met on the football field.'

The Revd J.W. Marsh of Nelson, Lancashire – also Referee J.W. Marsh! (1907)

'They called me a poof, they called me orange and plenty of other insults that you could not print in a newspaper. They were being particularly vitriolic, but I just kept my head down. What can you do? They are morons.'

Crystal Palace owner Simon Jordan on an enjoyable visit to Ashton Gate!

'The baby is due is due on 5 June, but it's bound to come about 12 o'clock on 24 of May when the play-off final is about to start. I'm looking forward to it coming. It's going to be good fun, but it's weird at the moment because you've got all the excitement of football, so with the baby, I'm all over the shop.'

Lee Johnson – surely set to follow in his dad's footsteps as a quotable legend

'You deserved your win.'

Bill Shankly apologises to the triumphant City players after tipping Leeds to beat the Robins in the FA Cup fifth round, 1974

'I'm Bertie Banks, City's penalty king so I'm going in for nothing.'

City star Bert Banks – 20 goals in 44 games – informs a doorman he is entering a city centre night spot gratis!

He was eventually allowed access on the premise he would score a hat-trick in his next game away to Bolton – he did exactly that in a 5–0 win! (February 1903)

'It is something that has always been brought up, and there is no favouritism as far as Lee is concerned. We have had a policy and a way of selecting our teams all the way through the season and none of that changes for this game. I pick teams for the right reasons and the right occasions and if somebody misses out then that is unlucky. Everybody receives the same treatment. I think what we have got is a group of sixteen players who deserve to be in that group of sixteen.'

Johnno puts the record straight about son Lee

BONUS!

The triumphant Bristol City squad that won promotion in 1975/76 were rewarded with £1,000 bonus cheques. The lucky players were: Cashley, Gow, Merrick, Tainton, Ritchie, Collier, Drysdale, Cheesley, Sweeney, Mann, Gillies, Whitehead, Brolly, Fear, Emanuel and Harding.

Boss Alan Dicks pocketed £5,000 for guiding the Robins back to the top flight.

HOP SCOTCH

City's record against clubs north of the border is fairly average with just four wins out of eleven games. The complete list of results, including cup matches and friendlies, is:

Ayr United 2–1 City
Celtic 1–1 City
Clyde 1–1 City
Clydebank 1–4 City
Clydebank 3–0 City
East Fife 4–3 City
East Fife 0–2 City
City 5–3 Hibs
Hibs 1–1 City
Partick Thistle 2–0 City
City 3–0 Partick Thistle

THE LUCKY TAM-O'SHANTER

When City drew the all-conquering Leeds United side for an FA Cup fifth-round tie at Ashton Gate, more than 37,000 fans packed into the Robins' ground to see a potential cup upset. Despite falling behind to a goal from Billy Bremner, Gerry Gow levelled the scores and earned a replay at Elland Road. Played on a Tuesday afternoon and watched by a crowd in excess of 47,000, the result was believed to be a foregone conclusion, but against all odds, Gillies scored for City in the 73rd minute sending 8,000 City fans wild. That proved to be the only goal of the game and was City's greatest Cup win for twenty-nine years. As the champagne flowed in the dressing room, Gillies was mobbed by jubilant City fans and left without any clothes, save for a Tam-O'Shanter borrowed from Gerry Sweeney to cover up his particulars! The Scottish hat then became the Robins' lucky mascot, though Liverpool ended the epic run in the quarter-finals with a 1–0 win at Anfield.

NEW YEAR'S WOE

City don't traditionally start the New Year in spectacular fashion, as a rule, winning just seven of twenty-eight fixtures played on he first day of the New Year. In fact, after winning their very first 1 January match by beating Blackpool 1–0 in 1903, City wouldn't taste victory in the League again for almost seventy years when a 1–0 win over Birmingham City ended the jinx. In between, there was a Gloucestershire Cup win over Bristol Rovers 4–0 in 1927, but from 1974 to 1990, City failed to record a win on this day, though in 2001 a 6–2 win over Cambridge United was the first New Year's Day win for a decade.

City's complete New Year's Day record is:
Pld 29   W 8   D 5   L 16   F 37   A 51

EIGHT TOO MUCH?

In 1968, two City players played in the number eight shirt after substitute Derrick, wearing a number eight jersey instead of the number twelve shirt he should have been wearing, replaced Garland who was, of course, wearing the number eight shirt. Neither the referee nor the Oxford United players noticed, but if Garland had been booked and Derrick then picked up a yellow card when he came on, he'd have been then shown a red and sent off! But neither were, so there was no early bath, even if it would have made this story more interesting.

SHANKS FOR THE MEMORY

City took on Bill Shankly's teams on eight occasions, though the majority were during his time as manager of Huddersfield Town. The first meeting was at Ashton Gate in October 1956, when City beat Huddersfield 2–1, though the Terriers won the return meeting by the same score. Huddersfield won 3–1 at City the following season (1957/58) with a 0–0 draw at Leeds Road later in the campaign. With a young Denis Law leading the line for the West Yorkshire outfit, the Robins won 1–0 away in September 1959 and won the return at Ashton Gate 2–1 a week later. Shankly's last match in charge of Huddersfield saw him oversee a 6–1 home win for his team before he moved on to begin a fifteen-year career as Liverpool manager. The only time City faced Shankly's Liverpool was in 1974, when his team ended an epic Robins FA Cup run at the quarter-final stage.

After seeing off the mighty Leeds United in the previous round, John Toshack scored the only goal of a tight game at Ashton Gate to end the Wembley dreams of thousands of Bristolians.

City's complete record against Shankly is:

Pld 8   W 3   D 1   L 5   F 8   A 14

HONOURABLE MENTIONS . . .

City's proudest moments, so far, have been:

Division Two champions 1905/06
Division One runners-up 1906/07
FA Cup runners up 1909
Division Three (South) champions 1922/23, 1926/27, 1954/55
Welsh Cup winners 1934
Anglo Scottish Cup winners 1977/78
Freight Rover Trophy winners 1986
Freight Rover Trophy runners-up 1987
Auto Windscreen Shield runners-up 2000
LDV Vans Trophy winners 2003

CLIFTON CAN'T BRIDGE GULF

City's first ever FA Cup tie – as Bristol South End – was played during the 1897/98 season with a first-round victory over Clifton. The Robins recorded a resounding 9–1 win with Carnelly bagging four of the goals. The team that day was: Monteith, Davey, Sinclair, Mann, Higgins, Hamilton, Wylie, Carnelly, Cale, O'Brien and Russell.

City then won 5–2 away to Trowbridge in the second round before being beaten 2–0 away to Southampton in the third round. In fact, City would fail to progress past the third round for their next eleven attempts, but when they finally did, they went all the way to the final, losing 1–0 to Manchester United at The Crystal Palace. After, that, it was back to business as usual with City failing to get past the third round for the next seven years.

SHOT DOWN

Aldershot might have won the 1946/47 curtain-raiser 4–3, but City were to have the last laugh. The Robins recovered to remain unbeaten in the next thirteen Division Three South games but were in the middle of a sticky patch when the Shots arrived in Bristol for the return fixture. City put their Hampshire opponents to the sword in emphatic style, recording a 9–0 win – a club record that is yet to be surpassed.

It was the Robins' only win in eight matches and though they finished the division's top scorers with 94 goals, it was QPR and Cardiff City who won promotion to Division Two while City had to be content with third place.

FREE VIEW RESTRICTIONS

City missed out on a lot of revenue during their time at their first ground, St John's Lane. A hill overlooking the ground became the perfect platform for hundreds of supporters to watch their matches for free and it became known as 'Mutton Hill'. The club eventually erected a 30ft high sheet to block the view which became an early forerunner for advertising hoardings.

MASCOT DE-CIDER

The club's mascot, Scrumpy the Robin, owes much to the south-west region's obsession for cider. He's been the club's mascot since 2005, with rumours that the previous incumbent was last seen in the city centre, drowning his sorrows and playing The Wurzels on his iPod.

City Cat used to rule the roost and purr his way around Ashton Gate before home games, but he was forced to retire when Scrumpy arrived on the scene. Having two mascots was considered until it was pointed out that cats and robins generally don't mix all that well!

WURZEL SCRUMMAGE

The club's official anthem is 'One For The Bristol City' by The Wurzels. First released in 1976, it is the tune the team run out to at home matches. A newly recorded version of the song reached number 66 in the UK charts in September 2007.

Another Wurzels classic, often heard at Ashton Gate is 'I am a Cider Drinker'. Here are the lyrics to one of their most successful ditties:

When the moon shines on the cow shed
And we're rollin' in the hay
All the cows are out there grazing
And the milk is on its way

Chorus
I am a cider drinker
I drinks it all of the day
I am a cider drinker
It soothes all me troubles away
Ooh aargh ooh argh aay

It's so comely in the kitchen
The smell of rabbit stew
When the breeze blows past the farmyard
You can smell the cow sheds too
When those combine wheels stops turning
And a hard day's work is done
There's a pub around the corner
It's the place we have our fun

Chorus
I am a cider drinker
I drinks it all of the day
I am a cider drinker
It soothes all me troubles away
Ooh aargh ooh argh aay

Now dear old Mabel, when she's able
We takes a stroll down lover's lane
And we'll sink a pint of Sproffey
And we'll play old nature's game
But we end up in the duck pond
The pub is sized to close

With me breeches full of tadpoles
And the newts between me toes

Chorus
I am a cider drinker
I drinks it all of the day
I am a cider drinker
It soothes all me troubles away
Ooh aargh ooh argh aay
Ooh aargh ooh argh aay (repeat x3)

LET CIDER BE THE SPICE OF LIFE!

(© The Wurzels)

A GAME OF, ER, FOUR HALVES . . .

In 1918, Ashton Gate hosted a somewhat unusual event for the time – a baseball game between USA and Canada. Some 2,000 people saw the Americans triumph 6–5, though this was a one-off occasion. The locals' request that the cheerleaders be allowed to stay sadly fell on deaf ears.

ONLY CITY . . .

City entered the 1933/34 Welsh Cup as an invited guest. The Robins entered the tournament at the sixth-round stage, by which time such forces as Flint, Bala and Towyn had all been eliminated. The draw pitted City with one of the strongest sides left in the competition

– Cardiff City – but a 2–2 draw brought the Bluebirds back to Ashton Gate where they were beaten 1–0. A trip to North Wales followed and again, City held hosts New Brighton to a 2–2 draw before putting the Welsh minnows to the sword at Ashton Gate, 2–1. So seriously was the comeptition taken that the semi-finals were held on neutral grounds. Tranmere beat Bangor City and City edged past Port Vale 1–0 in a match played at Chester. The Robins now faced Tranmere Rovers at Wrexham's Racecourse Ground in the final, but the teams fought out a 1–1 draw meaning a return to Sealand Road, Chester, where City triumphed 3–0 to take the Welsh Cup for the first – and only – time. For the record, here are the stats for the final ties:

Welsh Cup Final: 24 April 1934 at the Racecourse, Wrexham:

Bristol City 1   **Tranmere 1**
Molloy   Clasper

City: Scattergood, Roberts, Taylor, Morgan, Parker, Brinton, Banfield, Molloy, Riley, Loftus, Scriven
Ref: S.F. Rous (Watford)
Att: 4,922

Replay: 3 May 1934 at Sealand Road, Chester:
Bristol City 3   **Tranmere 0**
Riley (2)
Scriven

City: Scattergood, Roberts, Birks, Morgan, Carter, Brinton, Homer, Molloy, Riley, Loftus, Scriven
Referee: R.A. Mortimer (Huddersfield)
Att: 4,000

The Robins declined the chance to defend the trophy the following season but Tranmere took part and this time went on to win the cup. City returned to the competition in 1936/37 but dipped out at the first hurdle, losing 2–1 at home to Swansea Town. A year later they were thrashed 6–2 by Newport County as the appeal of the Welsh Cup began to wane, somewhat.

THEY SAID IT. . .

'Sorry I'm late – I got lost on the flyover system.'
Alan Dicks arrives at Ashton Gate, poised to become the Robins' new manager in 1967

'There were seagulls and a nice harbour – and the sun was shining! It was just like being home in Bermuda!'
Shaun Goater arrives in the exclusive resort of Bristol from Rotherham in 1996

'I remember having the ball and being on the bus on the way back, and you know it kind of being a prized possession. I think my father still has it.'
Kevin Mabbutt recalls his hat-trick away to Manchester United, October 1978

APRIL FOOLS?

Cellophane across the goals, two left boots for the striker, a tin of tartan paint on order for the dressing rooms and a referee without a pea in his whistle – it could only be April Fools' Day. The question is, how many times have City set themselves up for some dodgy headline or other over the years by playing on the first day of April? Well, City have played twenty-one times on this day throughout the club's history and done fairly well all told, losing just four times. All but one of those matches were League games, with a 2–0 Gloucestershire Cup win over Bristol Rovers on 1 April 1907 being the only exception. City's first game on April Fools' Day was a 3–1 defeat at Gainsborough Trinity and the latest fixture was a 2–1 home win over Yeovil in 2006.

The complete record is:

Pld 21   W 8   D 9   L 4   F 31   A 26

GOALS APLENTY

The City team of 1952/53 had plenty of goals in them, though they conceded a few, too. Every game they played during that campaign averaged three goals but it was on the season run-in that they excelled themselves in terms of good, honest entertainment during two cracking matches at Ashton Gate. In February against Torquay, City equalled their highest-ever scoring draw with the West Country cousins sharing eight goals in a 4–4 draw. Just over a month later, City repeated the feat again, drawing 4–4 with QPR at Ashton Gate. Three successive defeats in the final seven games meant City slumped to fifth place in the table, missing out on promotion to Division Two by just three points. The Robins have drawn 4–4 away from home on three occasions against Aston Villa (1907), Hull City (1964) and Notts County (1999).

FIRST NAME ON THE SHEET

Bristol City's all-time leading appearance holders in all competitions, bar the Gloucestershire Cup are:

John Atyeo (1951–66)	645
Louis Carey (1995–2004 & 2005–present)	625*
Trevor Tainton (1967–82)	581
Brian Tinnion (1993–2005)	551
Tom Ritchie (1972–81 & 1983–85)	504
Gerry Sweeney (1972–81)	490
Rob Newman (1967–82)	483
Gerry Gow (1969–81)	445
Scott Murray (1997–2004 & 2005–9)	437
Geoff Merrick (1967–82)	433
Ivor Guy (1946–57)	426
Mike Thresher (1954–65)	415
Jack Connor (1960–71)	408

* *correct as of 1/8/2012*

SONGS

'He's here, he's there, he's every f*****g where, Gerry Gow, Gerry Gow!'

The City fans' ode to the one and only GG

THE GOALDEN BOYS

It seems hard to believe that City have had just four players who have managed to score 100 goals or more for the club. Nobody can predict the future, but it seems safe to say that John Atyeo's incredible scoring record for the Robins will never be beaten, as he is currently 219 goals ahead of anyone else. One name not on the list below but one that almost certainly would have been had he not moved to pastures new, is Shaun Goater. A prolific scorer outside the top-flight, 'the Goat' went on to score more than 100 goals for Manchester City after leaving Ashton Gate in 1998. Here are the Top 20 goalscorers who did stick around:

John Atyeo (1951–66)	351
Tom Ritchie (1969–81 & 1982–84)	132
Arnold Rodgers (1949–56)	111
Jimmy Rogers (1950–56 & 1958–62)	108
Alan Walsh (1984–89)	99
Scott Murray (1997–2004 & 2005–09)	92
Tot Walsh (1924–28)	91
John Galley (1967–72)	91
Brian Clark (1937–51)	89
Sammy Gilligan (1904–10)	87
Bobby Williams (1958–65)	82
Don Clark (1937–51)	77
Glyn Riley (1982–87)	77
Cyril Williams (1939–48 & 1951–58)	74
Lee Peacock (2000–04)	63
Billy Maxwell (1905–09)	61
Tony Thorpe (1998–2002)	61
Wayne Allison (1990–95)	59
Rob Newman (1981–91)	59
Gerry Sweeney (1971–82)	59

THE BEST OF TIMES, THE WORST OF TIMES . . .

Here is a list of some notable City records:

Record League win — 9–0 versus Aldershot FC (28 December 1946)

Record FA Cup win — 11–0 versus Chichester City (5 November 1960)

Record League defeat — 0–9 versus Coventry City FC (28 April 1934)

Highest attendance — 43,335 versus Preston North End (16 February 1935)

Most League appearances — 597 John Atyeo (1951–66)

Most League goals scored — 314 John Atyeo (1951–66)

Most goals scored in a season — 36 Don Clark (1946–47)

Record transfer fee paid — £2.25m paid to Crewe Alexandra for Nicky Maynard, July 2008

Record transfer fee received — £3.5 million from Wolverhampton Wanderers for Ade Akinbiyi, July 1999

Record sequence of League wins — 14 – 9 September 1905 to 2 December 1905 – (a joint League record)

RED, RED ROBINS

City's record against Manchester United probably stands up against almost anyone's in England having avoided defeat in 20 of the meetings between the two teams. The first ever clash between the clubs was in September 1901 when United, then known as Newton Heath, won a Division Two fixture 1–0. The highest profile meeting was the 1909 FA Cup final, won by United 1–0. Manchester United have beaten City just 15 times in 35 attempts, with the Robins winning 10, the last of which was an unforgettable Kevin Mabbutt hat–trick at Old Trafford in October 1978. That 3–1 win for Alan Dicks' team was City's last triumph in this fixture, though the teams have not met competitively since February 1980.

The complete record against United is:
Pld 35   W 10   D 10   L 15   F 39   A 48

Biggest win: 4–0 (1902)

Heaviest defeat: 1–5 (1905)

Biggest League win: 4–0 (1902)

Heaviest League defeat: 1–5 (1905)

Biggest home gate v Man Utd: 28,783

'ACCRINGTON STANLEY – WHO ARE THEY?'

A 1980s TV commercial for milk came up with the phrase above, but Bristol City fans would have justification for uttering those words with City only ever meeting Accrington twice competitively. The teams – thankfully – have never shared a division but met in the 1957/58 season in the FA Cup third round. Drawn away, City settled for a 2–2 draw in Lancashire before dispatching Accrington 3–1 in the replay at Ashton Gate watched by an impressive gate of 32,196 – who said Stanley weren't a big draw?

AN A–Z OF CITY PLAYERS

Nathan Abbey may only have played once for City before moving to the giddy heights of life with Torquay United, but he stayed just long enough to distinguish himself in one respect – he's the first name in any historical alphabetical list of City players. Arriving on a free transfer from Leyton Orient in February 2006, Nathan stayed for just six months before moving to Plainmoor on another free transfer. Dele Adebola is second from the front, with the last player in the list being Clemens Zwijnenberg, who stayed on loan for a month from Danish side Aalborg in September 1998.

Some City fans reckon Zwijnenberg also has the distinction of being one of the worst players to have ever pulled on a City shirt and therefore justifies his place at the bottom of the pile.

TOFFEE KNOWS

One of the Premier League's longest-serving managers, David Moyes, made 109 appearances for the Robins between 1985 and 1987. The future Preston and Everton boss arrived from Cambridge United for a modest fee of £10,000 and would leave for Shrewsbury for £25,000 two years later. A Scottish youth international, defender Moyes scored 10 goals while at Ashton Gate.

CITY SLICKERS

City's best-ever league finish came in the club's sixth season – the 1906/07 campaign. City finished three points behind champions Newcastle United to finish runners-up in the old Division One, the Premier League of its day. With just seven games to go, the title looked as though it might be heading back to Bristol for the first time. A win at St James's Park against title rivals Newcastle would mean the Robins would be virtually home and dry, but in front of 40,000 Geordie fans, the Magpies won comfortably 3–0. Worse was to follow as City then lost to Bolton and Aston Villa at Ashton Gate before winning the last four games, but alas it was too late. Still, it remains the club's proudest season to date and finishing above the likes of Liverpool, Manchester United, Aston Villa and Arsenal isn't something every club can boast. The final table was:

DIVISION ONE 1906/07

		HOME						AWAY				
	Pld	W	D	L	F	A	W	D	L	F	A	Pts
Newcastle Utd	38	18	1	0	51	12	4	6	9	23	34	51
BRISTOL CITY	38	12	3	4	37	18	8	5	6	29	29	48
Everton	38	16	2	1	50	10	4	3	12	20	36	45
Sheffield Utd	38	13	4	2	36	17	4	7	8	21	38	45
Aston Villa	38	13	4	2	51	19	6	2	11	27	33	44
Bolton W	38	10	4	5	35	18	8	4	7	24	29	44
Arsenal	38	15	1	3	38	15	5	3	11	28	44	44
Man Utd	38	10	6	3	33	15	7	2	10	20	41	42
Birmingham City	38	13	5	1	41	17	2	3	14	11	35	38
Sunderland	38	10	4	5	42	31	4	5	10	23	35	37
Middlesbrough	38	11	2	6	33	21	4	4	11	23	42	36
Blackburn R	38	10	3	6	40	25	4	4	11	16	34	35
Sheffield Wed	38	8	5	6	33	26	4	6	9	16	34	35
Preston NE	38	13	4	2	35	19	1	3	15	9	38	35
Liverpool	38	9	2	8	45	32	4	5	10	19	33	33
Bury	38	9	4	6	30	23	4	2	13	28	45	32
Man City	38	7	7	5	29	25	3	5	11	24	52	32
Notts County	38	6	9	4	31	18	2	6	11	15	32	31
Derby County	38	8	6	5	29	19	1	3	15	12	40	27
Stoke City	38	7	6	6	27	22	1	4	14	14	42	26

ABANDONED GAMES

There have been eleven occasions on which City have had competitive matches abandoned owing to varying reasons; some with more dramatic repercussions than others. In November 1901, City travelled to Bristol

Rovers for an FA Cup Fourth Qualifying Round tie and were losing 2–0 with 10 minutes to go when thick fog descended – there was a sharp increase of City fans going to church the following day! The rearranged match was 116 minutes old – deep into extra-time in fact – when the ref called a halt to proceedings owing to bad light. Rovers eventually won the tie 3–2.

A month later and City's home league match with Gainsborough Trinity was stopped due to bad light with the Robins 2–0 ahead.

In 1935, fog was again the culprit when City were drawing 1–1 with Crystal Palace with 83 minutes played and in 1957 the Robins led 1–0 at Anfield before the ref stopped play at half-time.

An FA Cup fourth-round tie at Leicester City was also called off at half-time with the score 0–0 and on Boxing Day 1963, QPR trailed 3–0 at Ashton Gate in a Division Three clash and ten years later a Division Two game at Sheffield Wednesday lasted 55 minutes before the referee decided the pitch was unplayable – the score was 0–0.

A full-house at Ashton Gate were enjoying a thunderous game with Leeds United in December 1976, but with thick fog shrouding the stadium from the tenth minute onwards the game at least managed to last until half-time with the score still goalless.

Perhaps the most memorable of all the abandoned games was the January 1994 FA Cup third round clash with Liverpool. Having gone behind to an Ian Rush goal, Wayne Allison levelled the scores and City were pushing for a win when floodlight failure brought matters to a close. The game was replayed and, bizarrely, Ian Rush again opened the scoring for Liverpool before Wayne Allison equalised! The Groundhog Day scenario ends there with the game this time reaching a natural conclusion. The replay at Anfield will live long in the memory of any City fan who witnessed it as Brian Tinnion's spectacular long-range shot settled matters to give the Robins a famous 1–0 win.

The last game involving City to be called off during play was the 2002 home match against Notts County which lasted 49 minutes before the ref had seen enough. Not many in the 10,696 crowd were too bothered, with the Robins trailing 1–0.

The complete record of abandoned games is:

P11   W 3   D 6   L 1   F 8   A 6

The results of the re-arranged games are:

P 11   W 5   D 1   L 5   F 19   A 17

SENT TO COVENTRY

City's record league defeat came on 28 April 1934 when they lost 9–0 away to Coventry City during a Division Three South game. The Sky Blues notched up an amazing seventy goals at home that season and managed a hundred in total – the result at Aston Gate? A goalless draw of course!

LIKE SENDING COLE TO NEWCASTLE

Andy Cole became the Robins' record signing in March 1992 when he moved to Ashton Gate from Arsenal for a fee of £500,000. Many believed that, after eight goals in twelve games towards the end of the 91/92 campaign, Cole's goals had kept the club in Division Two and the money paid had been well spent.

The razor-sharp Cole then gave a glimpse of what was to come during his first full season with City, notching a goal just 28 minutes into the first game of the season against Portsmouth and he added another at Luton the following week. He then scored a hat-trick in the League Cup tie with Cardiff City to confirm his cult status among City fans.

After a knee injury kept him out for a month, Cole then found his shooting boots again, scoring in six successive league games taking his tally into double figures, but managed just one goal in the next twelve games. Then, after pledging to score the goals to keep City in Division One, a bid of £1.75m from Newcastle United for Cole was accepted and the future England striker was transferred to St James's Park.

He had scored a total of 24 goals in 45 matches for the Robins and his sale represented a 250 per cent profit on his original transfer fee. He may have just been passing through, but while he was a Robin, Cole was red hot!

LEAGUE POSITIONS

The club has taken part in the English League since 1901 – here's how they've have fared in the table over the years:

Season	League	Final Position
1901/02	2	6th
1902/03	2	4th
1903/04	2	4th
1904/05	2	4th
1905/06	2	1st
1906/07	1	2nd
1907/08	1	10th
1908/09	1	8th
1909/10	1	16th
1910/11	1	19th
1911/12	2	13th
1912/13	2	16th
1913/14	2	8th
1914/15	2	13th
1919/20	2	8th
1920/21	2	3rd
1921/22	2	22nd
1922/23	3 (South)	1st
1923/24	2	22nd
1924/25	3 (South)	3rd
1925/26	3 (South)	4th
1926/27	3 (South)	1st
1927/28	2	12th
1928/29	2	19th
1929/30	2	19th
1930/31	2	16th
1931/32	2	22nd
1932/33	3 (South)	15th
1933/34	3 (South)	18th
1934/35	3 (South)	15th
1935/36	3 (South)	13th
1936/37	3 (South)	16th
1937/38	3 (South)	2nd

1938/39	3 (South)	8th
1946/47	3 (South)	3rd
1947/48	3 (South)	7th
1948/49	3 (South)	16th
1949/50	3 (South)	15th
1950/51	3 (South)	10th
1951/52	3 (South)	15th
1952/53	3 (South)	5th
1953/54	3 (South)	3rd
1954/55	3 (South)	1st
1955/56	2	11th
1956/57	2	13th
1957/58	2	17th
1958/59	2	10th
1959/60	2	22nd
1960/61	3	14th
1961/62	3	6th
1962/63	3	14th
1963/64	3	5th
1964/65	3	2nd
1965/66	2	5th
1966/67	2	15th
1967/68	2	19th
1968/69	2	16th
1969/70	2	14th
1970/71	2	19th
1971/72	2	8th
1972/73	2	5th
1973/74	2 (old)	16th
1974/75	2 (old)	5th
1975/76	2 (old)	2nd
1976/77	1 (old)	18th
1977/78	1 (old)	17th
1978/79	1 (old)	13th

1979/80	1 (old)	20th
1980/81	2 (old)	21st
1981/82	3 (old)	23rd
1982/83	4 (old)	14th
1983/84	4 (old)	4th
1984/85	3 (old)	5th
1985/86	3 (old)	9th
1986/87	3 (old)	6th
1987/88	3 (old)	5th
1988/89	3 (old)	11th
1989/90	3 (old)	2nd
1990/91	2 (old)	9th
1991/92	2 (old)	17th
1992/93	1 (old)	15th
1993/94	1 (old)	13th
1994/95	1 (old)	23rd
1995/96	2 (old)	13th
1996/97	2 (old)	5th
1997/98	2 (old)	2nd
1998/99	1 (old)	24th
1999/2000	2 (old)	9th
2000/01	2 (old)	9th
2001/02	2 (old)	7th
2002/03	2 (old)	3rd
2003/04	2 (old)	3rd
2004/05	League 1	7th
2005/06	League 1	9th
2006/07	League 1	2nd
2007/08	Champ	4th
2008/09	Champ	9th
2009/10	Champ	10th
2010/11	Champ	15th
2011/12	Champ	20th

THE ASHTON GATE EIGHT

Not a group of prisoners wrongly accused of a crime, more eight footballers who helped ensure that Bristol City Football Club continued to operate beyond 1982.

When club finances were announced to be close to £1m in the red, the receivers hovered, ready to move in and, in all likelihood, lock down Ashton Gate for the last time. However, in a desperate bid to save City, two local businessmen, Deryn Coller and Ken Sage, launched an initiative to raise £1m in shares, but the plan depended on eight senior squad members accepting redundancy packages.

The octet of seasoned pros were all on lengthy contracts and high wages and there would be no way the new set-up could continue to operate with such huge overheads but the players had signed legally binding contracts and had their rights, too. They were offered £58,000 each, but the PFA negated an improved deal of £80,000 each plus a testimonial, which was accepted.

The players were Chris Garland, Peter Aitken, Jimmy Mann, Julian Marshall, Gerry Sweeney, Geoff Merrick and Trevor Tainton and their departure signalled the end of Bristol City as it had once been and heralded the new organisation running the club known as Bristol City (1982). The fans rallied for the first game under the new regime and, featuring a team of raw young talent nicknamed 'The Bristol Babes', they saw City draw 0–0 at home to Fulham in front of a gate almost double the size of their average for the season. The Ashton Gate Eight, meanwhile, left for pastures new.

ON YER BIKE!

During the 2003/04 campaign, City fan Jer Boon cycled to every first-team game the Robins took part in, raising more than £10,000 for the Breast Cancer Campaign in the process. Boon, 35, clocked up more than 7,000 miles over the course of the season, but his last ride to Cardiff to see City take on Brighton at the Millennium Stadium, ended in disappointment as the Seagulls won 1–0.

THE GLOUCESTERSHIRE CUP – THE EARLY YEARS

City first took part in the Gloucestershire Cup as Bristol South End on 25 January 1896, losing 4–0 to Eastville Rovers. Though many local league sides have taken part in the competition, eventually the tournament became an annual one-off game between City and Rovers. As far back as 1899 the match drew great interest, with 11,433 people watching that particular final played at St George and won 2–1 by the Robins. In 1903 a total of more than 20,000 fans watched City and Rovers meet three times in sixteen days and after the first two games ended in draws, Rovers triumphed 4–2 in the third game at Ashton Gate. In 1907, Rovers easily had their best crowd at home to City in the Gloucestershire Cup, with 12,629 turning out to see City win 2–0 at Eastville.

With City reaching the 1909 FA Cup Final, the tournament was held over until the following season and City then won two finals in the space of 10 weeks!

GREEN BEHIND THE GILLS

When Gillingham began the 1926/27 season with a 1–1 home draw against City, they couldn't have imagined what was in store in the return game. The Robins recorded their biggest score and highest match aggregate when the teams met again in January winning 9–4! City were dynamite at home that season, winning 19 of their 21 home League games but the next game after Gillingham saw a rather more sombre 1–0 win at Watford before another goal-fest at home, beating Crystal Palace 5–4. Unsurprisingly, the Robins were crowned Division Three South champions at the end of the season.

JOBS FOR THE BOYS

Several former City players have surnames that were also jobs or professions. They are: Albert Fisher, William Bailiff, Jimmy Baker, Phil and Stan Barber, C. Butcher and finally Charles, Tony and W. Cook.

BRISTOL SOUTH END

Milford Road, Southville, may not register immediately with most City fans as an address of any importance, but in early spring 1894, in a house owned by Fred Keenan, Bristol South End were formed in principal – a club that would eventually become Bristol City FC. Few clubs' origins can be traced back to a particular day and time, but when eighteen men were invited to Keenan's house on 12 April at 7.30 p.m., ideas were put forward, opinions expressed and by the end of the meeting a new club existed in Bristol. Money was pledged to the tune of almost £7 to cover administration costs and four days later a committee was formed with Harry and Ted Locke sharing the duties of being treasurers and one of Eastville Rovers founders W.B. Hodgkinson became secretary and W.R. Nurse was elected chairman. These men meant business and just twelve days after the first historic meeting at Milford Road, news came that Bristol's latest football club was now up and running. The team, it was announced, would play in red shirts and navy blue shorts but there was resistance among local officials and membership to the Bristol and District League was turned down flat – owing to the club's lack of history!

If those officials expected South End to duly roll over and die, they couldn't have been more wrong. The men behind the fledgling club had one goal – to make Bristol South End the biggest club for miles around and after securing a home ground at St John's Lane, Bedminster, a list of attractive friendlies were drawn up to bring the club firmly into the spotlight and with the backing of the Gloucestershire FA, they would also be able to take part in English and Amateur Cup competitions.

BSE's first game was also backed by the people of Bristol and on Saturday 1 September, the club played its inaugural game against West of England champions Swindon Town. More than 3,500 intrigued spectators watched Swindon triumph 4–2 but South End had well and truly arrived – much to the chagrin of Bedminster, who had seen several of their players move over to the new club. In 1897, still considered to be the runt of the litter, Bristol South End became Bristol City in order to gain admission to the Southern League, but the new club had even greater ambition. For the start of the 1900/01 season, City and bitter rivals Bedminster merged and Ashton Gate became City's new home. The slightly revised colours were red shirts and white shorts. Elsewhere, from the ashes of Eastville Rovers, Bristol Rovers had formed and the city now had two prominent clubs who divided Bristol into red and blue halves, though City have always had the lion's share of support – and nothing has changed over a century later!

LET THERE BE LIGHT!

In 1952, inventor and club chairman Harry Dolman spent the summer months working in his factory at Pennywell Road, Euston, designing the first set of floodlights for Ashton Gate. After being commissioned for £3,500, Dolman's floodlights were no more than tall metal poles with clusters of lights fixed to the top. On 27 January 1953, the floodlights were turned on for the first time at a City home game – a friendly against Wolverhampton Wanderers – a groundbreaking event in the history of football in Britain. Though Wolves won 4–1, a bumper crowd of 24,008 had turned out for the novelty of a match played at night and more lucrative friendlies were organised soon after against Cardiff City and East Fife, both of which proved box-office winners with the supporters.

UPS AND DOWNS

City have won ten promotions and been relegated ten times since the inaugural 1901/02 League season. In 1921/22 City finished bottom of Division Two and the following season they won promotion from Division Three South as champions – only to finish bottom of Division Two again the following year! That yo-yoing pales into insignificance with the disastrous slip from thirteenth in Division One (then the top league) in 1979 to three successive relegations to Division Four, even managing to slump to the bottom of the lowest League for a period. Arguably, City are only now starting to recover from that awful three years between 1979 and 1982.

PLAY-OFF WOES

Don't mention the word 'play-offs' to any City supporter after five unsuccessful attempts in the club's history. The wretched play-off luck began in 1987/88, when, after finishing fifth in the old Division Three, City beat Sheffield United 1–0 at home before drawing 1–1 at Bramall Lane. That set up a final with Walsall and after the first leg ended 3–1 to the Saddlers, it seemed Joe Jordan's side had missed their chance, but City redressed the balance with a thrilling 2–0 victory at Fellows Park to level the aggregate scores. Back then, games weren't settled on penalties or away goals and after losing a shoot-out to decide where the replay was, City failed to repeat their heroics and slumped 4–0 in the third match between the clubs. In 1996/97, the Robins finished in fifth position, but fell at the first play-off hurdle after losing 2–1 in both the home and away legs against Brentford. In 2002/03, third place in Division Two wasn't good enough to win promotion for the Robins and again they failed to make the play-off final, losing 1–0 at Cardiff City and then drawing a tense second leg 0–0. A year later and City again finished third in Divsion Two, after drawing the first leg of the semi-final against Hartlepool 1–1, the teams reconvened at Ashton Gate for the second leg. Adam Boyd gave the visitors the lead and with 88 minutes on the clock, it seemed the Monkey Hangers were on their way to the Millennium Stadium, but City somehow managed not only to equalise, but score a second in added time to win 2–1. The final against Brighton was a disappointing affair, with the Seagulls triumphing 1–0. Perhaps the most galling of all the play-off final defeats, however, was saved for the 2007/08 campaign. City had finished fourth in the Championship, one place below Hull City. The Robins had to overcome Crystal Palace if they were to win a place in the final, set to be staged at the new Wembley Stadium. A 2–1 win at Selhurst Park, followed by a 2–1 win at Ashton Gate set up a final against Hull City with the prize a place in the Premier League. After an absence of twenty-eight years from the top flight, the City fans travelled to London with high expectations, particularly as Hull had never been in the top division in their history. Sadly, Dean Windass scored the game's only goal leaving Gary Johnson's side crestfallen – let's hope when City eventually do win promotion from the Championship, it's because they've finished in the top two and gone up automatically. Play-offs? You can keep them!

GOALMOUTH SCRAMBLE

Club legend John Atyeo was not just a fantastic player who scored numerous cracking goals, he also kept the majority of City players and staff supplied with fresh eggs from the chickens he kept at his Dilton Marsh home! Rumours that he delivered the eggs in a shell-suit are, thankfully, untrue.

THE HAIRDRYER TREATMENT

Yes, Alex Ferguson once played for City – though not the Alex Ferguson that went on to manage Manchester United to one or two trophies. City's Alex Ferguson, a goalkeeper, arrived from the inauspicious surrounds of Newport County in 1946 at the ripe old age of forty-one, made 33 appearances and then left for Swindon Town 16 months later.

ANIMALS, ETC.

Several players have had surnames that could have doubled as animals, birds or fish. Shaun Lamb, Walter Moles, Ray Fox, Ernie and Lee Peacock, Scott and Dave Partridge, Shaun Goater, R. Pollack and Ivor Fish . . . the latter, sadly, was never paired up front with G. Fry.

JUST NOT CRICKET . . .

Despite signing from Arsenal for a fee of £4,000, outside-right Arthur Milton had already decided that, despite winning one England cap, his future lay in cricket rather than football. Chairman Harry Dolman signed Milton regardless and he went straight into a City side destined for promotion to Division Two. He played 14 times for the Robins and was never on the losing team, but after promotion had been secured, Milton confirmed he was to concentrate solely on a career as batsman with Gloucestershire. On his Test match debut against New Zealand, Milton hit 104 not out, proving his decision had probably been correct. Milton is the last player to play for England at both football and cricket and after his retirement as a player aged twenty-seven, City reclaimed half of the transfer fee they had paid Arsenal.

HIGHEST FINISH

The Robins' 1906/07 campaign remains the most successful to date. City finished second in their inaugural season in the top flight and it remains the club's best finish in nine attempts at life in England's premier division. City lasted five seasons in Division One from 1906 to 1911 and it would be another sixty-five years before they returned. The Robins' best modern-day finish was in 1978/79 when Alan Dicks' side achieved a respectable thirteenth place finish before being relegated the following season. City have been absent from the top division since 1980 and have never played in the Premier League.

FEED THE GOAT!

Shaun Goater gained instant cult status at Ashton Gate during his all-too-brief stay. The Bermudian striker had cut his teeth in the lower leagues with Rotherham United but in his biography, *Feed the Goat*, he admitted that the former mining town and constant leaden skies depressed him somewhat. When City paid the Millers £150,000 in 1996 for his services, Goater arrived in Bristol, saw the sea, listened to the seagulls and immediately felt at home! 'Goat', as he became affectionately known, scored on his League debut against Gillingham – albeit a 3–2 defeat – and quickly formed a Caribbean connection with Barbados-born winger Greg Goodridge. By the end of his first season, Goater, who had bagged two hat-tricks in his first season with the Robins, had managed 24 goals in 49 appearances in all competitions. A star was born!

Four games into the 1997/98 campaign and Goater was at it again, scoring his third hat-trick for City in a 3–0 home win over Wigan Athletic. He continued to poach with the instinct of a born goal-scorer until the Robins lost 2–0 at Plymouth Argyle on 21 March 1998. Thereafter came a shock £400,000 bid from relegation-threatened Manchester City which was accepted by City, much to the dismay of the Ashton Gate faithful. Though the Goat's departure arguably cost the Robins the Division Two title (though not promotion), and he exchanged divisions as Man City were relegated to the third tier of English football for the first time, Goater was instrumental in helping the Blues back to the Premier League. It was fitting that such a popular footballer should end his career at Ashton Gate – though in the colours of Southend United – and that he receive an ovation from not only Shrimpers fans, but Bristol City – and several hundred Manchester City fans on a day to remember for all in attendance. Goat scored 42 goals in 87 games for the Robins – a fantastic record.

RUN OVER A BLACK CAT?

City suffered their worst home defeat since 1949 when they lost 6–1 to Sunderland in 1990 in the League Cup. Despite the Robins leading 1–0 from the first leg at Roker Park, the Black Cats arrived in Bristol for the second leg to mark the appointment of new boss Jimmy Lumsden. Though Hauser gave Sunderland a first-minute lead, Nicky Morgan levelled the scores on the night just four minutes later. City would go on to register ten shots on target during the game, but failed to score another goal, while the visitors managed just seven shots on target all evening – and six of them went in! Definitely not City's night. . . .

FIRST LEAGUE SEASON

City's inaugural League campaign kicked off in 1901 after the club won a place in Division Two for the first time. The first match was on 7 September away to Blackpool and City won 2–0 with Paddy O'Brien scoring both goals. The club's first home League game at Ashton Gate was a 3–0 victory over Stockport County – one of thirteen wins out of seventeen home games in Bristol.

Only five defeats in the last six matches prevented City from taking third place – they finished instead in sixth, just two points off third.

Billy Jones, Billy Tuft and John McLean were ever-presents and Joe Connor and Bert Banks were the top scorers with ten goals apiece.

The final table 1901/02 was:

	P	W	D	L	F	A	W	D	L	F	A	Pts
1. West Brom	34	14	2	1	52	13	11	3	3	30	16	55
2. Middlesbrough	34	15	1	1	58	7	8	4	5	32	17	51
3. Preston NE	34	12	3	2	50	11	6	3	8	21	21	42
4. Arsenal	34	13	2	2	35	9	5	4	8	15	17	42
5. Lincoln City	34	11	6	0	26	4	3	7	7	19	31	41
6. BRISTOL CITY	34	13	1	3	39	12	4	5	8	13	23	40
7. Doncaster R	34	12	3	2	39	12	1	5	11	10	46	34
8. Glossop NE	34	7	6	4	22	15	3	6	8	14	25	32
9. Burnley	34	9	6	2	30	8	1	4	12	11	37	30
10. Burton Utd	34	8	6	3	32	23	3	2	12	14	31	30
11. Barnsley	34	9	3	5	36	33	3	3	11	15	30	30
12. Port Vale	34	7	7	3	26	17	3	2	12	17	42	29
13. Blackpool	34	9	3	5	27	21	2	4	11	13	35	29
14. Leicester City	34	11	2	4	26	14	1	3	13	12	42	29
15. Manchester Utd	34	10	2	5	27	12	1	4	12	11	41	28
16. Chesterfield	34	10	3	4	35	18	1	3	13	12	50	28
17. Stockport C.	34	8	3	6	25	20	0	4	13	11	52	23
18. Gainsborough T	34	4	9	4	26	25	0	2	15	4	55	19

PIRATE INVASION

Following a 1–1 draw with Leyton Orient, Bristol Rovers' Eastville South Grandstand was destroyed by a fierce blaze, leaving their ground unsafe to play football and without changing rooms. While emergency repairs were undertaken, City offered Rovers the use of Ashton Gate for their home games and from 30 August 1980 until 27 September 1980, Rovers played five matches at their temporary home.

Ironically, the game before their tenure at Ashton Gate was a 0–0 draw with City – at Ashton Gate! Despite Rovers' poor form, they drew all three League games they played at City's home ground, drawing with Grimsby, Oldham and Newcastle United and beat York City 1–0 and drew 0–0 with Portsmouth in the League Cup.

Curiously, after four clean sheets in the five games they played during that spell, the only other clean sheet they kept at home that season was during a 1–0 win over Chelsea at Eastville – maybe they should have stayed in the red half of Bristol longer!

The Pirates' record at Ashton Gate was:
Pld 5   W 1   D 4   L 0   F 3   A 2

ROBIN ATTACKS SWAN

When City boss Gary Johnson ran on to the pitch in 2007 to 'tackle' Swansea's irritating Izzy Iriekpen who had been preventing a Robins free-kick at a crucial point in the game, the referee consigned Johnno to the stand for the remainder of the game. The game ended 0–0 but Bristolian poet Gareth Calway recalled the incident in a poem he wrote for the *Western Daily Press*. He wrote:

> We are West Country blokes. We have
>   humble-grumble hopes.
> We make self-depreciatory jokes. We are
>   always on the ropes.
> When we win we think it's a hoax. Our
>   striker bursts through – then he croaks.
> Now we are really close, to those dizzy second
>   tier slopes.
> As second to those country folks, from
>   Scunthorpe United (who aren't such dopes).
> We deserve some master-strokes. And this
>   man who's managed to coax.
> A side that goes second and copes. Has been
>   sent off for wanting it most.
> More than time-waters and soft yolks.
>   Dressed in black and think they're Popes.
> And turn games into soaps.
> Our Big City team always gropes. While
>   many a lesser team lopes,
> But this one could be the toast 'Promotion
>   and Championship hosts'.
> And we're hymning deep in our throats. And
>   we don't want it gone up in smokes.
> Gary gets to his heart and stokes. Don't send
>   him off – hug him close.

NAME GAME

Hardly surprisingly, the most common surname to play for City is Smith. Jones and Williams are the only other two names to rack up double figures – the complete list is:

Smith	14
Jones	13
Williams	10
Brown	9
Wilson	8
Morgan	7
Thompson	6
Turner	6
Edwards	6
Taylor	6
Davis	5
Hughes	5
Johnson	5

There really was, as the song went, only one Dariusz 'Jacki' Dziekanowski, however!

KOP THAT!

City have one of the most impressive records against Liverpool in the country. Of the 34 meetings between the clubs in League and Cup, the Robins have triumphed 13 times, drawing a further five games. Though the Merseysiders have won 21 of the clashes, City have won eight of the 15 League games at Ashton Gate and have recorded four wins at Anfield. The last League meeting between the clubs was in March 1980 and the last FA

Cup clash was City's famous 1–0 win at Anfield in January 1994, courtesy of a Brian Tinnion thunderbolt.

AMERICAN SCREAM

City's 1973/74 pre-season tour saw a disastrous trip to the USA where a mixture of bad planning and hapless hosts combined in equal measure to see what had been an exciting looking adventure turn into a few weeks of disappointment and frustration. It began with an embarrassing 2–1 defeat to Baltimore Bays, though things improved with a 4–1 win over Cincinnati, but planned matches against Boston and Washington fell through, leaving the players to take part in 5-a-side games back at their Baltimore base before flying home to England.

CAESAR'S SALAD DAYS

He came, he saw, but he didn't conquer, rather buggered off to Airdrieonians. That City should sign a player voted by Arsenal fans as the worst to ever represent their club, speaks volumes for the Robins' problems in the early 1990s. It would be difficult to say Gus Caesar was well past his best, as according to Gunners fans, nobody had seen his best, but nonetheless, Caesar played 13 games during a calendar year at Ashton Gate before moving north of the border. His career demise was rapid and up to 2001 he was playing for Hong Kong Rangers. Still, at least Gus can claim to have played for City and Arsenal, which ain't so bad, is it?

TIME, GENTLEMEN?

Plans to replace the pub made famous by its legendary landlord Billy Wedlock with nineteen flats were met with anger from Bristol City Supporters' Trust. Built in 1900, the former Star Inn on Ashton Road was renamed Wedlock's when City and England star Billy Wedlock became its landlord and he lived and worked at the pub for forty-three years.

A Bristol landmark, particularly for the supporters of the Robins, the pub has been in existence for more than a century. In February 2009, plans were announced to demolish the pub to make way for flats. More than 1,000 people signed a petition to keep the pub as a resource for the community with the Victorian Society joining the fight to save the building. English Heritage decided not to list Wedlock's meaning there was little to stop developers other than public opposition. . . .

WHEN WILL I BE FAMOUS, MR CHAIRMAN?

Former City chairman Scott Davidson was once a member of 1980s boy band Bros whose hits include 'When Will I Be Famous' and 'I Owe You Nothing'. Davidson, who held the chair at Ashton Gate from 1996 to 2001, was also a keyboard player with the Pet Shop Boys.

ON A ROLL

City's best ever run of League wins came during the 1905/06 Division Two season when they, unsurprisingly, were eventually crowned champions. City had begun the campaign with a 5–1 defeat to Manchester United at Newton Heath but then won their next eight games by a single goal, adding another six victories to complete 14 wins on the bounce. They remained unbeaten in 24 matches all told and only suffered one more defeat – 2–1 at home to Leicester City – all season.

LEGEND: GERRY GOW – 'THE ASHTON GATE GROWLER' (1969–80)

Gerry Gow cut his teeth – and his legs, head and most other parts of his body – marauding in City's midfield for the best part of eleven years after joining the club as an apprentice in the late 1960s.

His mop of wild, curly hair gave him a dishevelled, unkempt look that was entirely in keeping with his image on the pitch. Gow was one of football's real hard men, but unlike a number of others of his ilk, he could play football, too. Nobody messed with Gerry Gow and if you did, then watch out, because he'd come back and hit you harder, particularly if you happened to be wearing the colours of Bristol Rovers or Cardiff City. If you were the quarry, you'd better be somewhere else – and quick.

His career at Ashton Gate was one of understatement. He got on with his job, got paid, had a few jars and went home. Consequently he became something of a best-kept secret in the West Country, which was just the way Bristol City wanted it.

Gow was a terrace hero at Ashton Gate and only a fool would think he was nothing more than a hatchet man. He was a ball-winner, yes, but he had vision, was an excellent dead-ball specialist who could score goals and worked the Robins' engine better than Scotty on the Starship Enterprise. There was many an opponent when faced with Gow who would utter 'I cannae take any more captain'. He once ran the length of the pitch to become involved in a brawl with a Cardiff player who was giving a team-mate a hard time and was never far from any potential ruck, usually started by one of his no-holds-barred thundering challenges.

At 28, he'd done all he could with Second Division City. Apart from an Under-23 cap, the Glasgow-born grafter had been criminally ignored by Scotland for the past five years where the likes of Graeme Souness and Don Masson blocked his path. It was not going to be easy to raise his profile and find a top-flight club but when John Bond became Manchester City's new manager in October 1980, it was Gow he turned to first in order to give his struggling side a spine. City had dropped out of the top division and Alan Dicks had been replaced by Bobby Houghton; the new man wanted to generate funds to ignite his side and quickly climb the table. Only days into his tenure, Bond's offer of £200,000 for Gow was too good for Houghton to turn down. Sadly, Manchester City couldn't give him the kind of platform he must have been aspiring to for years, though inspired by Gow, they did reach the 1981 FA Cup Final, only to lose to Spurs. The following season, Gow struggled with injuries and was eventually sold to Rotherham United before finally hanging his boots up a couple of years later.

DERBY DAYS

City and Bristol Rovers have been battling out for the supremacy of the city for more than 100 years and the derby matches of today are no less intense than when they first began. Following City's transformation from Bristol South End to Bristol City, Rovers followed suit in February 1899 by changing their name from Eastville Rovers to Bristol Rovers and the first truly Bristol derby – in that both clubs now used Bristol in their club name and discounting the Gloucestershire Cup matches – was on 13 April 1900 in the Southern League Division One and was a 1–0 win for Rovers at Eastville.

On 27 November 1901, City and Rovers met in the FA Cup for the first time with City winning 3–2 at Ashton Gate. It would be another 21 years before the clubs met again, with their first League games at Division Three South level pulling in gates of 30,000 for each clash, with City winning at Eastville 2–1 and Rovers triumphing at Ashton Gate. In 1926/27, City recorded their highest aggregate victory over Rovers in the League, winning 5–0 at Eastville and 3–1 at home – but Rovers avenged those thrashings by recording their highest aggregate League double, winning the 1933/34 curtain-raiser at Ashton Gate 3–0 and then making Robins fans even more miserable by winning the return game 5–1, 8–1 overall.

During wartime, the clubs met in a two-legged FA Cup tie, with City winning their home leg 4–2 and the away leg 2–0 to progress with a 6–2 aggregate. When the League resumed again in 1946/47, it was City who had gathered together a stronger squad while Rovers were left with a threadbare team destined to struggle. City won 3–0 away and 4–0 at home and completed another League double the following year, winning 2–0 at Eastville and 5–2 at Ashton Gate – happy days! Rovers' 2–1 win at Ashton Gate in 1950 was the Robins' first home defeat to their deadliest rivals for 15 years and Rovers repeated the feat the following season, not knowing that it would be almost 35 years before they would again record a League victory at City's home ground. The 1952/53 campaign was the first time there were no goals in either fixture, but the 1957/58 season was packed with goals – 3–2 for City at Ashton Gate, 3–3 in the return and a 4–3 win at Ashton Gate for Rovers in the FA Cup.

City recorded their first League double for 15 years, winning both Division Three fixtures in 1962/63. There were three successive goalless draws between the clubs between 1976 and 1981 – the clubs had been in different divisions for four years and during 1981/82 both Bristol clubs were relegated to Divison Three. Ironically, sandwiched in those intervening years, City recorded 3–1 and 6–1 wins over Rovers in the Anglo-Scottish Cup.

In 1984, following City's incredible drop from the top division to the foot of the lowest league, the Robins managed to cheer their fans by beating Rovers on their own patch in the FA Cup – probably the only time City caused a cup shock in Bristol! The teams were paired together again the following year and Rovers exacted their revenge, winning 3–1 at Ashton Gate. The club slugged it out in the League and League Cup in 1991/92, both winning the home League clashes but the League Cup saw City win the first leg 3–1 and then somehow lose 4–2 at home to crash out on the away goals rule. City's last League double over Rovers was in 1997/98, winning 2–1 at the Memorial Ground and 2–0 at Ashton

Gate – City also saw off the Pirates 2–1 over two legs in the League Cup, too. The last meeting of any kind between the clubs was in February 2007, with Rovers winning a Johnstone's Paint Trophy semi-final 1–0 on aggregate over two legs.

The total records are:

League:

	Pld	W	D	L	F	A
City	88	34	30	24	126	108
Rovers	88	24	30	34	108	126

FA Cup:

	Pld	W	D	L	F	A
City	8	5	1	2	15	11
Rovers	8	2	1	5	11	15

League Cup:

	Pld	W	D	L	F	A
City	4	2	1	1	7	6
Rovers	4	1	1	2	6	7

Other Cup Competitions (not Gloucs Cup):

	Pld	W	D	L	F	A
City	8	5	1	2	19	6
Rovers	8	2	1	5	6	19

Total:

	Pld	W	D	L	F	A
City	108	46	33	29	167	131
Rovers	108	29	33	46	131	167

RECORDS AGAINST ROVERS

Biggest win: 6–1

Heaviest defeat: 1–5

Biggest League win: 5–0

Heaviest League defeat: 1–5

Biggest home gate v Rovers: 39,583

Lowest home gate v Rovers: 1,175

Highest away gate v Rovers: 35,324

Lowest away gate v Rovers: 1,376

ASHTON GATE

Sitting in the Ashton Gate area of Bristol and with the magnificent backdrop of the Clifton Suspension Bridge, Ashton Gate was originally the home of Bedminster FC until the merger between City and Bedminster in 1900. Until then, City played their home games at St John's Lane and the merged team alternated between the two grounds until Ashton Gate become the permanent home of Bristol City FC in 1904. With a capacity today of 21,500, City's home has seen rugby and baseball matches, was a temporary home for Bristol Rovers and is one of the oldest grounds in the country.

The Atyeo Stand was opened in 1994, a year after City's greatest player John Atyeo died. Sponsored by Blackthorn, the Atyeo Stand is an all-seater single-tiered stand, which houses the dressing rooms and a large gym. Prior to this, there was terracing. At the opposite end of the ground is the Wedlock Stand (or the 'East End' to Robins fans), named after the legendary Billy Wedlock. It once exclusively housed away supporters, but the club, keen to generate a better atmosphere at that end of the ground, split the stand into home and away sections and is currently home to around 1,200 City fans, nicknamed the 'East End Ultras'.

Along one side of the pitch is the Dolman Stand, which is divided into an upper and lower area and is named after former City chairman and President Harry Dolman. Built in 1970, the lower part is used as a family area and opposite is the Williams Stand, built in 1958 and the current home of the directors' box and press box.

JOHNNO SAID IT...

'You cannot afford to sign the first player who becomes available in case Roy of the Rovers comes knocking on your door further down the line.'

Johnno – ever the comic

'It was an honour to get closer to Britney Spears than any man's managed before!'

Johnno (2003) – then Yeovil Town boss – on the same day his picture was placed alongside a revealing photograph of Britney Spears in a national newspaper

'I really feel for Brooks but thankfully he is only 26 – despite looking 36 – and has age on his side.'

Johnno comments on Yeovil's Ryan Brooks

'We had a big chat with the lads yesterday. We started by congratulating them, cuddling them, and saying well done for their performance at Coventry.'

Johnno shows his softer side. . .

BILLY'S BOOTS

City's first England international was striker Billy Jones who was selected after bagging 26 goals in 62 appearances for the Robins during the 1899/1900 season. He made his international debut on 9 March 1900 as England took on Ireland at Southampton. Jones also had the distinction of being the first City player to be awarded a benefit match with City taking on Third Lanark in 1903, earning him a not unsubstantial £102 in proceeds.

THE 1909 FA CUP STORY

If there's one chapter of City's history that's worth going to town on, it's the club's one and only appearance in the FA Cup Final. The Robins began their quest for glory in disappointing fashion against Division Two side Southampton, drawing 1–1 at Ashton Gate after missing a late penalty. City won the replay 2–0 at The Dell with Rippon successfully converting from the spot and Hardy adding a second. Next up were fellow Division One side Bury, a team City had already beaten 2–1 in the League, but again the Robins failed to see off their opponents at Ashton Gate and after a 2–2 draw, City had to travel north to win the replay 1–0 at Gigg Lane.

Norwich City were dispatched 2–0 at home courtesy of goals from Rippon and Burton and watched by an Ashton Gate crowd of 25,000 in the third round, but in round four – the quarter-finals – City were drawn away in the FA Cup for the first time since January 1906, taking on Glossop North End at Surrey Street.

The match should have been postponed as a blizzard gripped the area but with a full house already packing the ground, the game went ahead – how times have changed! City ground out a 0–0 draw in near-impossible conditions and then saw off Glossop side with a hard-fought 1–0 victory in the replay thanks to a goal from Sammy Gilligan. Another Derbyshire side, Derby County, were waiting in the semi-final at Stamford Bridge with Manchester United taking on Newcastle in the other game. City trailed 1–0 thanks to an early goal from the Rams and the epic cup run looked all but over with just seconds remaining. Dramatically, the Robins were then awarded a penalty in the last minute and Rippon expertly tucked the ball home to earn an unexpected replay at St Andrew's, home of Birmingham City four days later.

Derby again went ahead and again City levelled through a Rippon penalty just before the break and after dominating the second half, Hardy obliged with the winning goal to send thousands of Bristolians home in ecstasy.

With Manchester United winning their semi-final, the stage was set for a classic North v South final at The Crystal Palace in London. The talismanic Rippon was injured and despite playing the Reds at home and away in the space of four days a couple of weeks before the final and not conceding a goal in either game, it was defending League champions United who started the game as favourites.

With both sides' normal home kit being red shirts and white shorts, both decided to wear an alternative strip. United wore an all-white kit with a thin red line at the neck and wrists and City wore royal blue shirts and white shorts. Ironically, it was two former Manchester City players who proved the undoing of the Robins with the legendary Welshman Billy Meredith in mesmeric form and Sandy Turnbull scoring the only goal of the game. After both clubs reaped the profits of the 71,401 crowd, United commissioned a new ground to be built and a year later moved into their new home, Old Trafford – a stadium partly built with Bristol City fans' money!

Here are the all-important stats:

Round 1:
Bristol City 1–1 Southampton
Replay: Southampton 0–2 Bristol City
Manchester United 1–0 Brighton & Hove Albion

Round 2:
Bristol City 2–2 Bury
Replay: Bury 0–1 Bristol City
Manchester United 1–0 Everton

Round 3:
Bristol City 2–0 Norwich City
Manchester United 6–1 Blackburn Rovers

Round 4:
Glossop North End 0–0 Bristol City
Replay: Bristol City 1–0 Glossop North End
Burnley 2–3 Manchester United

Semi-Final:
Bristol City 1–1 Derby County
Replay: Derby County 1–2 Bristol City
Manchester United 1–0 Newcastle United

Final: Manchester United 1–0 Bristol City

Manchester United: Moger, Stacey, Hayes, Duckworth, Roberts, Bell, Meredith, Halse, Turnbull (J.), Turnbull (A.) Wall

Bristol City: Clay, Annan, Cottle, Hanlin, Wedlock, Spear, Staniforth, Hardy, Gilligan, Burton, Hilton

Referee: J. Mason (Burslem)
Linesmen: J.R. Schumacher (London), A. Green (Birmingham)

Attendance: 71,401

LADIES ONLY. . .

Bristol City Ladies were formed in 1990 and disbanded in June 2008. They reached the Women's FA Cup semi-final in 1994 and won promotion to the Premier League in 2004. Following funding problems, the majority of the senior squad moved to the University of Bath and currently play as Team Bath Ladies in the Southwest Combination Women's Football League.

ROBIN RED BREASTS

City's nickname 'The Robins' is relatively modern in that it can only be traced back to 1976. For eighteen years from 1976 to 1994, City sported a robin on the club crest, while the current badge is a simplified version of the Bristol coat of arms.

VAT MAN AND ROBINS

City's record transfer fee paid is £2.25m for Crewe Alexandra's Nicky Maynard. The Cheshire-born forward had been on Crewe's books since the age of seven but it wasn't until he was loaned out to non-League Witton Albion in 2006 that his star really began to rise and after continuing to impress for Crewe reserves on his return, he announced his arrival to senior football in spectacular style, scoring with his first touch against Millwall.

After 32 goals from 52 League starts, Maynard became one of the hottest properties in the lower divisions and in July 2008, he moved to Ashton Gate, taking on the coveted no. 10 jersey and promptly scored a hat-trick on his City debut against Royal Antwerp. Maynard failed to agree a new deal with City and in January 2012 he joined West Ham United for an undisclosed fee.

THE BIG TISSUE

During the 1972/73 season, tissue manufacturer Kleenex sponsored City's Man of the Match awards. Geoff Merrick won eight awards, while Trevor Tainton and Gerry Sweeney took half-a-dozen each. Peter Spiring was voted star man in five of his 24 starts and the next best was Gerry Gow with four.

RANDOM FACT

City's average gate during the 1952/53 was 17,758 while an average of 1,909 people watched the reserves.

ROBINS OFF TO A FLYER!

City have never started a league campaign in quite the same blistering home form they kicked off the 1947/48 with. City won their first six matches at Ashton Gate that season, scoring 26 and conceding just 2. That run included 6–0 victories over Southend United on the opening day of the season, Leyton Orient three weeks later and Norwich City three weeks after that! Yet despite winning ten out of the first 13 games, the Robins tapered off somewhat after Christmas and finished in seventh place.

CITY IN THE LEAGUE CUP – COMPLETE RECORD

The Robins have fared reasonably well in the League Cup and its various guises of Coca Cola Cup, Worthington Cup, Rumbelows Cup, Littlewoods Cup, Milk Cup and Carling Cup over the years and have twice reached the semi-final of the competition, only to lose on both occasions.

City's first game in the League Cup was in October 1960 which ended in a 1–1 draw at Aldershot. The most-played opponents are Nottingham Forest, with seven clashes and City have played Leicester City and Rotherham United five times in total. The complete record in the League Cup is as follows:

Total League Cup record:

Pld	Won	D	L	F	A
136	48	31	57	174	204

BRISTOL CITY MILESTONES

1894: Bristol South End formed and elect to play their games at St John's Lane, Bedminster.

1897: The club renames itself Bristol City and become a limited company following a meeting at the

Albert Hall in Bedminster. The new committee approach Woolwich Arsenal's Sam Hollis to be the club's first manager and after Hollis agrees to take over he is given a whopping budget of £40 (yes, £40) to assemble a squad capable of making a strong challenge in the Southern League.

1899: Bob Campbell takes over from Sam Hollis.

1900: City merge with rivals Bedminster FC. Bedminster, a professional club, play their home games less than a mile away from St John's Lane at Ashton Gate.

1900: City, made up of mainly Bedminster players, decide to play half their home games at St John's Lane and the rest at Ashton Gate.

1901: Sam Hollis returns to City and following the club's election to Division Two, leads them into their first season in the Football League. City win first game 2–0 away to Blackpool.

1901: The Robins return to St John's Lane to play their home games.

1901: Billy Jones becomes City's first England international.

1904: After three years at St John's Lane, City finally adopt Ashton Gate as their permanent home.

1905: Now a force to be reckoned with, City set a new Division Two record of fourteen consecutive League victories – a record that is shared with Preston North End and Manchester United and still stands to this day.

1905: Harry Thickett becomes City manager and leads the club to the 1905/06 Division Two title at the first attempt. The Robins win a club record thirty League games in the process.

1907: City finish runners-up to Manchester United in Division One – more than a century on, this remains the club's highest ever League finish.

1907: Central defender Billy Wedlock wins the first of his 26 England caps.

1908: Ashton Gate stages its first Rugby Union international as England take on Wales in front of a 21,000-strong crowd.

1909: City reach their first and only FA Cup Final, losing 1–0 to Manchester United at The Crystal Palace.

1910: Harry Thickett is sacked and replaced by caretaker boss Frank Bacon after City slump to the foot of Division One.

1911: Sam Hollis returns for his third spell as Robins' boss in January, but even he can't prevent relegation.

1913: Following the successful Rugby Union international of 1908, Ashton Gate stages an England home game, once again against Wales.

1916: Gale-force winds destroy Ashton Gate's South Terrace roof.

1920: City reach the FA Cup semi-final.

1922: The club returns to the lower leagues after relegation to Division Three (South).

1923: The yo-yoing between divisions begins as City win Division Three (South) title.

1924: City relegated again back to Division Three (South).

1927: After bagging 104 goals during the 1926/27 season, City are again crowned Division Three (South) champions. Tot Walsh grabs club record six goals in one match against Gillingham.

1928: After selling two players to Blackburn Rovers for a combined fee of £3,650, City are able to put a roof on the Winterstoke Road terrace.

1929: The Old Stand is partially destroyed by fire.

1932: City again relegated to Division Three (South).

1934: City win their first knock-out trophy after beating Tranmere Rovers to lift the Welsh Cup. Coventry City inflict a club record defeat, beating the Robins 9–0.

1935: Boom time at Ashton Gate where a record crowd of 43,335 watch the FA Cup tie between City and Preston North End.

1938: Despite finishing runners-up in Division Three (South), City fail to win promotion with only the champions going up to Division Two.

1941: The grandstand at Ashton Gate is totally destroyed during air raids over Bristol.

1945: After 3 hours and 22 minutes of a wartime cup match against Cardiff, City score a sudden-death winner – timed at 202 minutes!

1946: City return to League action in style, recording a club record 9–0 home win over Aldershot on 28 December.

1947: Don Clark sets new club scoring record by grabbing 36 League goals during the 1946/47 campaign.

1953: Ashton Gate sees floodlit football for the first time during a friendly with Wolverhampton Wanderers.

1955: City crowned Division Three (South) champions for the 1954/55 campaign and equal club record of 30 League wins in the process.

1960: Back to Division Three – minus the (South) – as the Robins ship 97 goals, lose 26 matches and generally endure an awful campaign.

1960: The green shoots of recovery begin as City thrash
Chichester 11–0 in the FA Cup – a record victory
in all competitions.

1965: Promoted to Division Two after finishing
runners-up in Division Three. City's new
floodlights are switched on for the first time
during a friendly against Wolves – the same
club the Robins played during Ashton Gate's
first floodlit game 12 years earlier!
The old set of floodlights was sold to Burton
Albion.

1966: Just three short of 600 League appearances
for City, club legend John Atyeo retires from
football.

1970: Harry Dolman, perhaps the most popular
chairman in City's history, is honoured by having
a stand named after him. The Dolman Stand cost
close to a quarter of a million pounds and came
complete with an indoor bowling green!

1971: City reach the semi-final of the League Cup –
the club's furthest foray into what was still a
relatively new competition.

1976: Alan Dicks' City side return to the top-flight
for the first time in 65 years after finishing
runners-up in Division Two.

1978: City win Anglo-Scottish Cup after dramatic
victory over Alex Ferguson's St Mirren.

1980: After four seasons in Division One, the Robins are relegated back to Division Two.

1981: The gloom worsens as City slump to a second successive relegation. . .

1982: Incredibly, City are relegated for a third successive season and at one point plummet to the foot of Division Four before relaunching as Bristol City (1982) Limited. The rescue package from two local businessmen saves the club from extinction in the nick of time.

1984: City begin their ascent back up the League by finishing third in Division Four.

1984: Terry Cooper becomes the club's oldest player to appear in a senior game, aged 40 years and 86 days.

1986: Just four years after almost going out of business, City lift Freight Rover Trophy at Wembley after beating Bolton Wanderers 3–0 in the final.

1987: The Robins almost defend their title as Freight Rover Trophy champions by reaching final for second successive year, only to lose on penalties to Mansfield Town.

1989: City are denied their third Wembley appearance in three years as they lose League Cup semi-final against Nottingham Forest over two legs.

1990: City move up another level after finishing Division Three runners-up and stacking up a club record 91 points in the process.

1992: Andrew Cole becomes City's record signing when the Robins pay Arsenal £500,000 for the striker's services.

1993: Newcastle pay £1.75m for Andrew Cole – a record transfer fee paid for a City player. Club legend John Atyeo dies.

1994: The John Atyeo Stand is completed at a cost of £1.8m.

1995: Everton's FA Cup fourth round tie at Ashton Gate results in City netting record receipts of £148,282.

1996: Scott Davidson becomes City's new chairman and a new board is employed.

1997: City lose 1997 Division Two play-off semi-final to Brentford by an aggregate of 4–2.

1998: City win promotion after finishing runners-up in Division Two.

1998: Ade Akinbiyi becomes the Robins' first million-pound signing when he signs from Gillingham for £1.2m.

1999: City's yo-yo reputation is further enhanced by relegation back to Division Two.

1999: Ade Akinbiyi leaves Ashton Gate for Wolverhampton Wanderers in a club record transfer deal of £3.5m, making him the most expensive signing ever outside the Premier League.

1999: Aged 16 years and 71 days, Marvin Brown becomes the youngest player to ever represent Bristol City in a senior game when he comes on as a substitute during a League Cup tie with Nottingham Forest.

2000: City reach final of Auto Windscreen Shield but lose 2–1 to Stoke City.

2002: Steve Lansdown becomes new chairman in October.

2003: City miss out on automatic promotion by three points and then lose to Cardiff City in the play-off semi-finals, losing 1–0 on aggregate.

2003: Solace comes to Ashton Gate in the form of a LDV Vans Trophy success after City beat Carlisle 2–0 at the Millennium Stadium, Cardiff, watched by almost 40,000 City fans.

2004: Long-serving Brian Tinnion makes his 500th appearance for City.

2004: Yet another season ends in heartbreak after City miss out on automatic promotion by just one point – this despite eleven successive League wins during December, January and February and boasting the best defensive record (with Doncaster Rovers) in the Football League. After beating Hartlepool over two legs, City played

Brighton & Hove Albion at the Millennium Stadium but lose 1–0. Danny Wilson is sacked and replaced by Brian Tinnion.

2005: Tinnion's City finish in seventh in his first season as manager. Despite missing out on promotion, some supporters are almost relieved the club won't be participating in the play-offs again!

2006: Brian Tinnion leaves City after club slump to a point off the bottom of the League. Gary Johnson leaves Yeovil Town to become the new boss.

2007: City are back in the Championship after a dramatic final-day victory over Rotherham United.

2008: The Robins' attempt to make it back-to-back promotions and win a place on the Premier League for the first time fails with yet another defeat in the play-offs. Playing at the new Wembley for the first time, City lose 1–0 to Hull City, courtesy of a Dean Windass goal.

2009: The Robins finish 10th in the Championship as they struggle to cope with the previous campaign's disappointment.

2010: Gary Johnson leaves after a disappointing season.

2010: Steve Coppell takes the hotseat, but after just four months, he quits the post stating a lack of passion for the game as a major factor behind his decision.

2010: David James becomes one of City's highest-profile signings. He stays for just two years before being released at the age of 42.

AND THE BAND PLAYED ON...

The Bristol City band's first full season at Ashton Gate started in time for the 2000/01 season, having originally appeared in February 2000, making their debut in an Auto Windscreens Shield quarter-final against Reading. Suitably inspired, City won 4–0 and the band became a regular feature at home games from then on. Revelling in their West Country roots, their most popular tunes are 'The Great Escape', 'I am a Cider Drinker', 'Combine Harvester', 'The Blackbird', 'One for the Bristol City' and 'Drink Up thy Cider'. The original line-up included David, Mark, John and Shaun on the drums, James (cornet), David (trumpet) and Paul (euphonium). The band can be contacted at bcfcband@hotmail.com.

BOXED OFF

The Robins have played 83 times on Boxing Day over the years with five of those games being friendlies and Gloucestershire Cup ties – all against Bristol Rovers. Of the 78 League games played on 26 December, the biggest City win came in 1914 when Grimsby were thrashed 7–0 in front of 11,000 Ashton Gate fans. City's worst defeat on this day has been by a margin of 5–0 – all away from home – with the first drubbing coming in 1936 against QPR and in 1955 and 1956 both Plymouth and Swansea beat the Robins 5–0, and a 5–2 loss at Derby the following year meant three successive Boxing Days had resulted in the opposition scoring five goals! Oxford United were the last side to hand out a five-goal defeat at the Manor Ground in 1973 while the only abandoned game was in 1963 with City leading 3–0 against QPR at half-time – typical!

The total League record on Boxing Day is:
Pld 79   W 26   D 23   L 30   F 127   A 122

CAPACITY CROWD

The four stands at Ashton Gate house a total of 21,477 fans. The Blackthorn Atyeo Stand holds 4,249 people; the Bristol Evening Post Dolman Stand holds 6,175 fans; the Prime Time Williams Stand can house 5,553 and the Bristol Trade Centre Wedlock Stand can accommodate 5,500 supporters.

BORN IN WEDLOCK

Billy Wedlock is City's most capped player with 26 England caps won between 1907 and 1914. He made his debut on 16 February 1907 aged 26 years and 109 days, and he scored his first goal – one of two he scored for England against Wales – in 1908. He also made his final appearance for his country against Wales in 1914.

BLOODY AMATEURS!

City's 1960 record win over Chichester is likely to stand for many more years. The FA Cup first-round thrashing of the Sussex minnows took place on Bonfire Night and it's fair to say their were one or two fireworks in the visitors' changing rooms at Ashton Gate that day. City won 11–0 with John Atyeo bagging five goals during the romp, though Chichester had originally been drawn to play the tie at home.

With their ground not quite up to scratch and a bigger pay day guaranteed in Bristol, the tie was switched and remains in the history books as the Robins' all-time biggest victory. City drew non-League opponents in the second round, too, but two King's Lynn goals in the final six minutes erased a 2–0 lead and a replay at Ashton Gate was needed to settle the affair. City won that 3–0 and Bobby Williams' solitary strike edged the Robins a little closer to Wembley with a 1–0 win over Plymouth Argyle.

After the initial fourth-round tie at Leicester City was abandoned because of a waterlogged pitch with the score at 0–0, City were rudely dumped out in the rearranged game, conceding five goals without reply at Filbert Street.

GOALS APLENTY

Few City fans could have imagined the 1926/27 Division Three South campaign would have been quite as entertaining as it eventually proved. Having narrowly missed out on promotion the previous season, the Robins kicked off with a 1–1 draw at Gillingham and won their first two home games by beating Newport County 4–1 and Watford 5–0, topping the table in the process. The goals continued to flow, especially at Ashton Gate but there was particularly satisfying 5–0 victory over Rovers at Eastville in October. However, a run of one win in five games and just five goals scored during November and December saw City drop to third – and out of the promotion places.

Two wins over Aberdare Athletic on Christmas Day and 27 December yielded nine goals and a 9–4 win over Gillingham ensured the perfect start to the New Year. Two five-goal salvos against Crystal Palace and Coventry City edged the Robins back towards the top of the table and following a 1–0 February win over QPR, City moved back to the summit of the division and remained there to win promotion having scored a club record 104 goals. They confirmed promotion and the title on the final day with a 3–0 win over Merthyr Town.

FA CUP MYSTERY

City adopted a philosophical approach to missing out on a money-spinning tie with Manchester United in 2008. The FA Cup third round draw saw the Robins pulled out of the hat and then former Arsenal star Sammy Nelson appeared to pull out no. 25 – United – but said it was no. 24 – Middlesbrough. Millions of viewers saw what appeared to be a fairly monumental error by Nelson but City were unconcerned about the fuss and accepted the FA's word that all was above board.

WALK LIKE AN EGYPTIAN

When is a record signing not a record signing? When his name is Emad Meteb, of course. A club-record deal of £1.5m was agreed for the Egypt international between the Robins and Al Ahly and the 25-year-old striker signed a three-year deal with City, but he angered club officials by going against their wishes before he'd even left Egypt! Meteb elected to turn out for his former club in the Cairo derby against Zamalek, despite being told not to by City, and leaving chairman Steve Lansdown to explain the deal was dead in the water: 'The Egyptian deal is off,' he said. 'To explain, the player passed his medical and agreed the deal, subject to getting a work permit. He couldn't sign officially until the work permit came through so he was allowed back to Egypt to sort that out and wave goodbye to the Al Ahly fans. He was clearly informed he could not play in the game against Zamalek and he went against that promise. We had second thoughts.'

NOT THEM AGAIN . . .

City have played in the FA Cup for more than a century, but some teams tend to crop up more than others, while several sides have never played the Robins in the most famous knock-out trophy in the world. Incredibly, one of the two teams City have faced more than any other happens to come from just a couple of miles away – Bristol Rovers. The Robins have played the Gasheads on no less than nine occasions, though the first two meetings were abandoned before their conclusion, once for fog and once for bad light. City have won three ties and Rovers were the victors in two.

Derby County just edge the overall record of FA Cup ties with the Robins and there have been some ding-dong battles between the clubs over the years. The first meeting was in 1909 in the FA Cup semi-final at Stamford Bridge, but the teams couldn't be separated after a 1–1 draw and a replay was arranged four days later at Birmingham City's St Andrew's stadium. This time, the Robins won 2–1 to progress to the final, though Derby gained a modicum of revenge by remaining unbeaten in the next four FA Cup clashes. The teams managed to avoid each other for 46 years after a 1934 triumph for the Rams at the Baseball Ground before being drawn out of the hat in 1980 for a third-round tie at Ashton Gate where a crowd of 13,384 saw City romp home 6–2. Ironically, they played each other at the same stage the following year, with the Robins grinding out a 0–0 draw at Derby before eliminating them again at Ashton Gate – the last time they met in the Cup – this time by a more sombre scoreline of 2–0 and almost 30 years have passed since the clubs last came out of the hat together. Bournemouth have played City eight times and have the edge overall with four wins and two draws and Liverpool have also played City eight times, though one of those games was abandoned due to floodlight failure. City have faced Cardiff City a total of seven times, while Notts County, Portsmouth and Aston Villa have all played the Robins half a dozen times, with Villa proving the kiss of death in the competition having failed to lose any of their ties with City. The other notable pairings have been Preston, Southampton, Nottingham Forest and Swansea, who have all played the Robins five times in the FA Cup.

BOGEY MEN

Aston Villa are one of the Robins' biggest bogey teams, though things have improved somewhat over the years. Want proof? How about this – City first met Villa in February 1900 and the tone was set as Villa won 5–1 and it would be 68 years and 18 matches before the Robins first tasted victory against the Midlands outfit – an incredible statistic. The historic victory came at Villa Park with a 4–2 win – this despite being 2–0 down after just nine minutes! Though City lost their next meeting, they then restored some sanity to the fixture by winning four successive games against Villa between 1969 and 1973. The teams have not met competitively since 1982.

The total record is (in all competitions):
Pld 38   W 8   D 10   L 20   F 38   A 59

CALLING THE SHOTS

City's longest FA Cup battle was with Aldershot when the two-evenly matched sides played each other four times before the FA Cup second-round tie was finally settled. Having already drawn 1–1 in the League six weeks earlier at Ashton Gate, it was clear there was little between the sides, despite Aldershot's lowly position in the Third Division. However, it seemed the Shots, who had a young Steve Claridge leading the line, were on their way to the third round after taking the lead on 76 minutes from a controversial penalty in the first meeting. Then, deep into injury time, Carl Shutt's weak header somehow beat goalkeeper Tony Lange to trickle over the line. The replay at Ashton Gate was a dull affair, ending 0–0 with Aldershot having the better chances – they at least won the toss for the second replay. In an amazing repeat of the first game, Shutt again equalised deep into injury time and even extra time couldn't separate the teams with the game ending 2–2.

The third replay, at Ashton Gate, saw Shutt strike again, but this time his tenth-minute strike proved enough for City to progress into the third round. City won the return League meeting 1–0 at the Recreation Ground and the Shots eventually ended bottom of the table and were relegated; that'll teach 'em!

RED, RED ROBINS

Way back when, the City fans used to sing the following song, either at Ashton Gate or on their way to away games. It was taken from the *Al Jolson Story* (Jolson recorded the song) and it was written by Harry Woods.

Apparently Charlton Athletic adopted the song, too, which is why it's not often heard these days. For those of you who fancy a bob down memory lane, here are the lyrics:

When the red, red robin comes bob, bob bobbin'
    along, along,
There'll be no more sobbing when he starts throbbing
His own sweet song.

Wake up, wake up, you sleepy head,
Get up, get up, get out of bed,
Cheer up, cheer up the sun is red,
Live, love, laugh and be happy.

What if I've been blue,
Now I'm walking through fields of flowers,
Rain may glisten, but I still listen for hours and hours.
I'm just a kid again, doing what I did again, singing a song,
When the red, red robin comes bob, bob bobbin' along.

THEY SAID IT...

'We've got a Polish inter-national! We've got a Polish inter-national!'

The City fans inform anyone who is listening that the gifted Dariusz Dziekanowski represented his country

'I was disappointed with Stern's involvement towards the end of the season and I left him out because I didn't feel he was giving us anything. Until you get to know that, you have to play him to see if he can give you the sort of game you are looking for.'

Stern words from Johnno after loan signing Stern John fails to impress

'In my heart I'd love to stay for another year but in my head I know I'll probably end up playing somewhere else next year. I'd like to stay local, but if I have to go abroad for a season or so then I'll do it. I have had a query from China and Australia as well.'

Scott Murray foresees the end of an era at Ashton Gate

'Ever since I've been at Bristol City I've been made to feel really welcome and this award shows how much people appreciate what I do, and I appreciate their support in return. I'm still talking to the manager and the chairman

about staying on at Bristol City, but if it comes to an end
I can safely say that this is a great club with a great set of
lads and great support.'

**City's Player of the Year 2009, Dele Adebola looks back
fondly on his time at Ashton Gate**

THE FERGIE FACTOR?

The design for the Robins' new stadium has been inspired
by none other than Manchester United manager Sir
Alex Ferguson. The architect in charge of designing the
planned 30,000-seat stadium at Ashton Vale discovered
Sir Alex's favourite stadium is Villa Park during an
informal chat, and those comments stayed with him as
he drew up plans for City's new home.

Mike Trice, of stadium designers HOK, has taken in
various aspects of Villa Park for the Ashton Vale project
because he believes the atmosphere will match that of
Aston Villa's home ground.

The new ground will herald a new era for the club and
will have the potential to expand its capacity to 42,000.

Trice, whose company has also designed Arsenal's
Emirates Stadium, the Millennium Stadium in Cardiff,
the new roof at Wimbledon's Centre Court, the new
Wembley and the 2012 Olympic Stadium, believes City's
new home will be one of the best he's ever created.

He said: 'We are trying to create all the benefits of a full
bowl and of different stands as well. Sir Alex holds Villa
Park in very high esteem because of the way the stands
are set up and we want to do the same thing here. It's a
good time to build now because builders are cheap, they
want work and a two-year contract is highly attractive.'

Sadly, at the time of going to press, the Ashton Vale project had been thrown into doubt after legal wrangles and objections from local residents at the proposed stadium site. By 2012/13, City were no closer to finding a new home to play at.

ANGLO-ITALIAN CUP

Initiated in 1969 as a contest for English and Italian league teams, the Anglo-Italian Cup was primarily invented as a reward to one of City's rivals, Swindon Town, who had won the English League Cup in 1969 but as a Third Division club were not allowed to enter the Fairs Cup (later UEFA Cup).

A curious competition that was open only to clubs in the second division of their respective leagues, it would appear under various monikers over the years without ever really catching fire, as such. Known first as the as Gigi Peronace Memorial, then the Anglo-Italian League Cup, both tournaments suffered through lack of interest from supporters and disciplinary problems.

In 1976 the tournament was revived and lasted 10 years, now known simply as the Anglo-Italian Cup before again fizzling out until 1992 when a final attempt was made to get the competition buzzing. With the final guaranteed to be played at Wembley Stadium, there was plenty to play for and City qualified for European competition for the first time in 1992/93 season after winning their domestic group phase of the Anglo-Italian Cup. The Robins narrowly beat Watford 1–0 at Ashton Gate and then held Luton Town 1–1 at Kenilworth Road to finish top of Group 5 and progress to European phase.

Group 5 results:

Bristol City 1–0 Watford
Watford 0–0 Luton Town
Luton Town 1–1 Bristol City

Table

	Pld	W	D	L	F	A	Pts
Bristol City	2	1	1	0	2	1	4
Luton Town	2	0	2	0	1	1	2
Watford	2	0	1	1	0	1	1

City then progressed into Group B, but failed to beat any of their Italian opponents home or away. After losing 2–0 at home to Cosenza, the Robins then lost an entertaining clash with Pisa 4–3 before crashing again at home, this time to Reggiana. Ironically, an impressive 2–2 draw with Cremonese was too little, too late and the Robins, when all the results for English and Italian sides had been totted up, were eliminated. City could at least take solace from the fact Cremonese went on to beat Derby County in the final.

Group B results:

Bristol City 0–2 Cosenza
Reggiana 0–0 Tranmere Rovers
Derby County 3–0 Pisa
Cremonese 2–0 West Ham United
Cosenza 0–3 Derby County
Tranmere Rovers 1–2 Cremonese
Pisa 4–3 Bristol City
West Ham United 2–0 Reggiana

Bristol City 1–2 Reggiana
Pisa 0–1 Tranmere Rovers
Derby County 1–3 Cremonese
Cosenza 0–1 West Ham United
Reggiana 0–3 Derby County
Tranmere Rovers 2–1 Cosenza
Cremonese 2–2 Bristol City
West Ham United 0–0 Pisa

Italian Table:

	Pld	W	D	L	F	A	Pts
1. Cremonese	4	3	1	0	9	4	10
2. Pisa	4	1	1	2	4	7	4
3. Reggiana	4	1	1	2	2	6	4
4. Cosenza	4	1	0	3	3	6	3

English Table:

	Pld	W	D	L	F	A	Pts
1. Derby	4	3	0	1	10	3	9
2. Tranmere	4	2	1	1	4	3	7
3. West Ham	4	2	1	1	3	2	7
4. Bristol City	4	0	1	3	6	10	1

1993/94

The following season the Robins again entered the Anglo-Italian Cup, but their opening domestic group result – a 3–1 defeat at Fratton Park – meant they had a mountain to climb in order to qualify for the European stages. A 2–1 win over Oxford United meant Portsmouth needed just a draw with Oxford at the Manor Ground in order to progress, though they actually won comfortably to eliminate both their opponents and City.

Group 4
Portsmouth 3–1 Bristol City
Bristol City 2–1 Oxford United
Oxford United 0–2 Portsmouth

	Pld	W	D	L	F	A	Pts
Portsmouth	2	2	0	0	5	1	6
Bristol City	2	0	0	1	3	4	3
Oxford United	2	0	0	2	1	4	0

After four years of effectively flogging a dead horse, the Anglo-Italian Cup was finally scrapped in 1996 after Genoa saw off Port Vale and seems unlikely to ever reappear – but you never know!

ZENITH DATA SYSTEMS CUP

City only played in the Zenith Data Systems Cup (which had formerly known as the Full Members' Cup and the Simod Cup) on two occasions, losing each time.

In the 1990/91 season, City drew 2–2 away to Oxford in front of just 1,323 supporters. Oxford won the resulting penalty shoot-out 3–2 and the following year City lost 2–1 at home to Southampton in the ZDS second round in front of a respectable 5,672 fans.

THE ASSOCIATE MEMBERS' CUP – COMPLETE RECORD

The Robins have taken part in the Associate Members' Cup – the trophy for teams of the bottom two leagues – since its inception in 1983 and have reached the final on four occasions, winning and losing twice. The AMC has had various sponsors over the years including Freight Rover, Auto Windscreens, Leyland DAF, Sherpa Van and Johnstone's Paints. The Robins' complete record is:

Season	Date	Opponent	Score	Comp	H/A	Att
1983/84	22 Feb 84	Exeter City	1–3	AM-1	A	1,040
1984/85	6 Feb 85	Hereford	1–1	AM-1(FRT)	A	2,690
1984/85	20 Feb 85	Hereford	1–0	AM-1(FRT)	H	3,446
1984/85	18 Mar 85	Port Vale	2–1	AM-2(FRT)	H	3,635
1984/85	25 Apr 85	Newport	1–2	AM-3(FRT)	H	3,167
1985/86	14 Jan 86	Plymouth	0–0	AM-Q(FRT)	H	2,402
1985/86	28 Jan 86	Walsall	2–1	AM-Q(FRT)	A	2,625
1985/86	27 Mar 86	Northampton	3–2	AM-SQF(FRT)	H	3,038
1985/86	16 Apr 86	Gillingham	3–0	AM-SSF(FRT)	H	5,707
1985/86	6 May 86	Hereford	0–2	AM-SF/1(FRT)	A	7,608
1985/86	9 May 86	Hereford	3–0	AM-SF/2(FRT)	H	11,558
1985/86	24 May 86	Bolton	3–0	AM-F(FRT)	N	54,502
1986/87	26 Nov 86	Exeter City	1–1	AM-Q(FRT)	A	1,338
1986/87	16 Dec 86	Bristol Rovers	3–0	AM-Q(FRT)	H	6,903
1986/87	27 Jan 87	Southend	1–0	AM-1(FRT)	H	4,195
1986/87	10 Feb 87	Brentford	3–0	AM-SQF(FRT)	H	7,425
1986/87	10 Mar 87	Gillingham	2–0	AM-SSF(FRT)	H	10,508
1986/87	8 Apr 87	Aldershot	2–1	AM-SF/1(FRT)	A	5,000
1986/87	14 Apr 87	Aldershot	4–1	AM-SF/2(FRT)	H	16,371
1986/87	24 May 87	Mansfield	1–1*	AM-F(FRT)	N	58,586

* lost 5–4 on pens at Wembley

1987/88	10 Nov 87	Swansea City	2–0	AM-Q(FRT)	H	5,037
1987/88	24 Nov 87	Wolves	1–3	AM-Q(FRT)	A	5,174
1987/88	19 Jan 88	Aldershot	0–1	AM-1(SVT)	A	2,662
1988/89	23 Nov 88	Bristol Rovers	0–1	AM-2(SVT)	A	3,940
1988/89	6 Dec 88	Exeter City	2–0	AM-Q(SVT)	H	3,642
1988/89	24 Jan 89	Wolves	0–3	AM-1(SVT)	A	14,216
1989/90	5 Dec 89	Swansea City	2–1	AM-Q(LDC)	H	3,488
1989/90	15 Jan 90	Reading	1–1	AM-Q(LDC)	A	1,784
1989/90	23 Jan 90	Notts County	0–1	AM-1(LDC)	H	4,902
1995/96	26 Sep 95	Oxford United	0–3	AM-Q(AWS)	A	2,558
1995/96	17 Oct 95	Barnet	2–0	AM-Q(AWS)	H	1,830
1995/96	28 Nov 95	Shrewsbury	0–0	AM-1(AWS)	A	2,258
1996/97	21 Jan 97	Swansea City	1–0	AM-Q(AWS)	A	5,600
1996/97	11 Feb 97	Watford	1–2	AM-Q(AWS)	A	3,142
1997/98	6 Jan 98	Millwall	1–0	AM-Q(AWS)	H	2,557
1997/98	27 Jan 98	Bournemouth	0–1	AM-Q(AWS)	A	2,124
1999/00	12 Jan 00	Cheltenham	3–1	AM-2(AWS)	H	4,123
1999/00	25 Jan 00	Bournemouth	1–1*	AM-3(AWS)	H	4,291
				* City win 4–1 on pens		
1999/00	15 Feb 00	Reading	4–0	AM-SSF(AWS)	H	8,733
1999/00	29 Feb 00	Exeter City	4–0	AM-SF/1(AWS)	H	12,742
1999/00	14 Mar 00	Exeter City	1–1	AM-SF/2(AWS)	A	2,929
1999/00	16 Apr 00	Stoke City	1–2	AM-F(AWS)	N*	75,057
				* at Wembley		
2000/01	5 Dec 00	Plymouth Argyle	0–3	AM-1(AWS)	A	1,364
2001/02	16 Oct 01	Torquay United	1–0*	AM-1(LDV)	H	3,407
				*City won on golden goal rule		
2001/02	30 Oct 01	Southend United	2–0	AM-2(LDV)	A	1,741
2001/02	4 Dec 01	Peterborough	2–1*	AM-3(LDV)	H	3,949
				*City won on golden goal rule		
2001/02	9 Jan 02	Bristol Rovers	3–0	AM-4(LDV)	H	17,367
2001/02	30 Jan 02	Cambridge U	0–0	AM-SF/1(LDV)	A	3,740
2001/02	19 Feb 02	Cambridge U	0–2	AM-SF/2(LDV)	H	12,264
2002/03	22 Oct 02	QPR	0–0*	AM-1(LDV)	A	4,722
				* City won 5–4 on pens		

2002/03	13 Nov 02	Boston United	2–1*	AM–2(LDV)	A	1,408

*City won on golden goal rule

2002/03	11 Dec 02	Wycombe	3–0	AM-3(LDV)	H	3,506
2002/03	21 Jan 03	Bournemouth	3–1	AM-4(LDV)	A	5,125
2002/03	18 Feb 03	Cambridge U	4–2	AM-SF/1(LDV)	H	7,173
2002/03	25 Feb 03	Cambridge U	3–0	AM–SF/2(LDV)	A	3,596
2002/03	6 Apr 03	Carlisle	2–0	AM–F(LDV)	N*	50,913

* at the Millennium Stadium, Cardiff

2003/04	14 Oct 03	Plymouth	0–4	AM–1 (LDV)	A	4,927
2004/05	29 Sep 04	Peterborough	1–0	AM–1 (LDV)	H	3,092
2004/05	2 Nov 04	MK Dons	2–1	AM–2 (LDV)	H	3,367
2004/05	30 Nov 04	Swindon	0–1	AM–3 (LDV)	A	7,571
2005/06	18 Oct 05	Barnet	2–3	AM–1 (LDV)	A	1,031
2006/07	1 Nov 06	Leyton Orient	3–1	AM–2 (JPT)	H	1,118
2006/07	29 Nov 06	Nottingham F	2–2	AM–QF (JPT)	A	4,107

* City won 4–2 on pens

2006/07	23 Jan 07	Brighton	2–0	AM–SF (JPT)	H	6,485
2006/07	21 Feb 07	Bristol Rovers	0–0	AM–AF 1/2 (JPT)	H	18,730
2006/07	27 Feb 07	Bristol Rovers	0–1	AM–AF 2/2 (JPT)	A	11,530

Bristol Rovers win 1–0 on agg

NO-BRAINER

Is it a myth or did it really happen? Joe Brain played for City between 1937 and 1939, playing 41 times and scoring 13 goals before leaving Ashton Gate to join Watford. When manager Bob Hewison was asked if he had any injury concerns for one particular weekend match, he told reporters, 'Well, I've got no Brain for a start.' It took the City boss about a millisecond to realise what he'd said, but, if the legend is true, it was, of course, too late!

THEY SAID IT...

'I've had enough!'
   Gerry Gow after missing his fourth penalty away to Aston Villa – he'd already seen efforts saved in games against Orient, Fulham and another penalty strike the outside of the post against Portsmouth, yet still ended the season with 13 goals

DOG GONE PUDDLES!

Picture the scene – QPR are taking on Bristol City at Loftus Road in a vital First Division match on 26 April 1977. Thinking of a pitch like a carpet with two teams playing velvety football? Think again – such was the torrential downpour in Shepherd's Bush that the game was in danger of being called off. The mudbath of a pitch was making playing conditions almost impossible and just when things seemingly couldn't get any worse, from somewhere, a dog ran on to the pitch. Worse still, the hapless pooch managed to get himself marooned in the middle of one of the huge puddles now covering the pitch – enter City star Geoff Merrick. Merrick saw the dog and managed to rescue him from a watery grave by carrying it to safety, much to the amusement of the 14,000 fans inside the ground. For the record, the game wasn't abandoned and the Robins won 1–0.

SUB SNUB

There are ways of getting an appearance fee and then there's John Palmer. With City boss Terry Cooper attempting to kill time in a match at Torquay United, Palmer got stripped and ready to come on with just seconds remaining. With the Robins leading 2–0, Palmer shook hands with the departing Paul Williams and just had time to step on to the pitch before the referee blew for full-time. The whole episode lasted no more than five seconds!

GREECE IS THE WORD

City embarked on a close-season tour of Greece prior to the 1973/74 campaign. In sweltering heat, the Robins began with an encouraging 1–1 draw with Olympiakos and repeated the scoreline against the lesser-known Agrinion. Alan Dicks' side wrapped up their tour with a 2–1 win against AEK Athens.

CULT HERO: DARIUSZ DZIEKANOWSKI

Dariusz Dziekanowski – 'Jackie' to one and all – was one of the most popular players to pull on a Bristol City shirt in the modern era. An enigma wrapped in a mystery, the words mercurial and maverick spring to mind in equal measure whenever his name is mentioned around Bristol. Jackie was an instant hit at Ashton

Gate, with City fans still in a state of shock that they'd managed to convince Celtic into letting him go for a paltry £250,000 fee. Jackie had played for the likes of Legia Warsaw and Widzew Łódz before moving to Parkhead and his sixty-odd Polish caps suggested he was a quality act. On his home debut against Southend United, Jackie missed a presentable chance after just one minute, but made amends later in the game by tucking away a Junior Bent cross on 67 minutes. It was almost two months before he next found the net, but when he did, he convinced any doubters what a class player he really was. Coming on as a second-half sub against Wolves, he smashed an 18-yard volley past Mike Stowell for his first goal six minutes from time and added a second three minutes later, dancing round the keeper to slot home his second, thus bringing an eleven-match winless run to an end. Suddenly the languid striker had rediscovered his spark and with Jackie pulling the strings, the Robins pulled away from the foot of the table by stringing an eight-match unbeaten run together. The vision, the passes, the deft touches, dummies and flicks had Ashton Gate eating out of the Pole's hands and he was, at times, simply breathtaking. Yet there were numerous times when he would frustrate and have his manager tearing his hair out, but woe betide the boss who takes on a terrace idol – both Jimmy Lumsden and Denis Smith lost their jobs while Dariusz Dziekanowski was in – or out – of the team and Russell Osman would be subjected to an almost unheard of protest by football fans. Undoubtedly Jackie's best performances came when he played alongside Andy Cole, a class act himself and a goal poacher *par excellence*. The pair struck up an instant understanding and when the Robins fired on all cylinders, it was invariably because Cole and

Dziekanowski were on song, too. With Cole's inevitable departure, Jackie's interest seemed to wane and his social life of late nights, nightclubs and fast cars began to catch up with him. Of course, he could do no wrong in the supporters' eyes, but new boss Russell Osman had seen enough. He saw Dziekanowski as a bad influence and whenever he was left out of the team, fans questioned his judgement. Even if the fans could have seen the wider picture, it's doubtful it would have made any difference. This was a player who lifted them collectively to a higher plane – a place they weren't used to and if Jackie did nothing for 89 minutes then produced a piece of sublime skill – be it a pass, trick or a goal – that was good enough for them. Osman knew he had to get rid of his wayward star before he cost him his job and at the start of the 1993/94 season, he shipped Jackie out of Ashton Gate for good. The supporters, thoroughly disgusted at Dziekanowski's departure, let Osman know exactly how they felt and when he scored against Southend just days later, the goal was greeted by stony silence. Osman lasted another 12 months before he, too, was shown the door.

LOSING FAITH

Gary Johnson made an inauspicious start to his career at Ashton Gate after inheriting Brian Tinnion's struggling outfit. Despite winning three of his first four League games, City then embarked on the worst losing run in the club's history, suffering nine successive defeats, seven in the League, one in the Football League Trophy and another in the FA Cup.

JOHNNO SAID IT...

'It is a little disappointing to find out we're away on the opening day, Boxing Day and the final day. We've got to make long journeys at the start and end of the season. We've got to make sure we give our supporters – who travel in big numbers – something to cheer about. Our away form last season was okay, so I suppose it isn't too bad in that case. We just need to improve our home form, turning those draws into wins.'

Johnno – unhappy with the 2009/10 fixture planners

'I very much hope Bristol becomes a host city if England and the FA win the right to stage the 2018 World Cup. Although it seems a long way off, it will soon come round and for our city to play a major role would be absolutely fantastic and would certainly live on long in the memory.'

Johnno looks to the not-too-distant future

'He came here on a free transfer and has been absolutely fantastic for us. We would like to keep him around for as long as we possibly can. He has been a major part of the success we have enjoyed over the last few years. He has had a wonderful Bristol City career and I will be doing everything I can to keep him here.'

Johnno heaps praise on Adriano Basso (2009)

JOHNNO v KEANO PART ONE – (THIS COULD RUN AND RUN)

'We did have discussions with his representatives. He's very close with Roy Keane and I think he'll end up with him. There was interest initially from us, but we pulled out very early.'

Johnno on the likely destination of winger Lee Martin

'There's a long way to go regarding Lee Martin and it's none of Gary Johnson's business. He should concentrate on signing his own players.'

Roy Keane's prickly response to Johnno's comments

THAT WAS THEN . . .

In these days of over-inflated transfer deals and huge wages, it's a sobering thought to think that when former Northern Ireland boss Peter Doherty (no, not the guy who is always in trouble with the police and fronts the band Babyshambles) was over the moon to agree a three-year deal worth a whopping £2,000 per YEAR! Cristiano Ronaldo probably earns that in an hour these days . . .

SUM TOTAL

At the end of the 2008/09 campaign, statto.com compiled an all-time table of English league clubs taking into account every league result from each club's inception. The good news is the Robins made the top 20 (Rovers were placed 53!) and were nine places higher than Chelsea. The top three are fairly predictable with Manchester United, Liverpool and Arsenal taking the first three berths.

City's total record to date is:

Home

Pld	W	D	L	F	A	GD
2146	1143	554	449	3767	2152	+1615

Away

Pld	W	D	L	F	A	GD
2146	523	559	1064	2367	3685	-1318

Total

Pld	W	D	L	F	A	GD	Pts
4292	1666	1113	1513	6134	5837	+297	5007

The Robins lie 43rd in the all-time FA Cup stats, trailing luminaries such as Darwen and Aldershot! Rovers are in 48th spot with the overall record as follows:

Pld	W	D	L	F	A	GD
283	113	69	101	443	386	+57

Finally, the Robins' League Cup record is the worst of the three domestic competitions, where they currently lie 55th in the all-time table.

The overall record is:

Pld	W	D	L	F	A	GD
140	48	34	58	176	207	-31

THE TWELFTH MAN

When the Robins gave the No.12 squad number to the City fans, they added a squad profile on the official club site which reads thus, 'Experienced members of the squad whose performance has been consistent throughout City's 104-year history, backing the club through good times and bad. Peaked with a 43,335 crowd in February 1935 for an FA Cup tie against Preston North End but current ground capacity means they currently average home gates of around 14,000. Remain one of the country's big hitters taking 40,000 to Cardiff's Millennium Stadium for the 2003 LDV Trophy final, 34,000 plus for the 2004 play-off final – also in Cardiff – and 36,000 to the 2007/08 play-off final against Hull City at Wembley. Tend to hit their best form during night games at Ashton Gate, although City's away support remains the envy of many clubs.

HAND(S) OF GOD?

Adriano Basso proved to be one of the most popular keepers of the modern era before he left the club after five enjoyable years in 2010. Here are a few things you might not know about the Brazilian shot-stopper:

Born: 18 April 1975

Birthplace: Jundiai, Brazil

He started his career with Ponte Preta before joining Atlético Paranaense

He moved to England to marry his wife

He spent three months on trial at Arsenal but wasn't
    offered a contract by the Gunners

He signed for St Albans in 2004 but moved to Woking
    later that season

He was spotted by City after 25 games for Woking and
    signed a few days into the 2005/06 season

He made his debut against Swindon Town during a live
    televised game

After overcoming initial doubts about his ability, he
    quickly became a huge crowd favourite

He is superstitious as well as a devout Christian –
    when his name is called over the PA, he always points
    to the sky – the City fans join in whenever
    this happens and along with Basso, say 'Always
    believe!'

The Bristol City Supporters Trust in partnership
    produced pointing foam hands with the words
    'Always Believe' on the front of them

He was crowned BBC West Footballer of the Year,
    BCFC Player of the Season and was nominated for
    the PFA Championship Team of the Season in
    2007/08

BASSO QUOTES

'To be honest many people don't understand or don't
believe. But I ask the Holy Spirit where they're
going to kick. He said "left" and I said "thank you."
I went to the left side and I saved the ball, so today
I was very blessed.'

**Devout Christian Basso has revealed that
divine inspiration helped him save a penalty against
Watford**

'I think it is a Brazilian attitude. One thing I put in my
mind is: "I don't leave my country to come here and go
back as a loser." And I don't leave my country to come
here and waste my time. I put my mind that every year
I should achieve something because if I don't achieve
anything one year, that's a waste of time.'

Basso's no time waster!

'I think as a Brazilian we never think to be second,
always looking to be first, always to win, always to be
in the top. For you to have this kind of mentality you
have to want to make something happen. Many times
people wait for something and say 'I'm going to see what
happens'. No, I didn't come here to see what was going
to happen, I came to make something happen. When
you understand that you are responsible for your future.
Nothing can stop you.'

**Basso reveals his determination
to succeed drives him on**

'Agents used to send DVDs to clubs to show them midfield players or strikers because they would get most money from them. Nobody was interested in selling goalkeepers. But because the clubs in Europe bought some players from watching films that were no good, they started sending people to watch games themselves. When they got there they saw some good goalkeepers so then started to bring them too. Now DVD doesn't work any more – too many times the director is Steven Spielberg but the player is no good!'

Basso reckons some players are edited to look better on the TV than in real life

'The problem is many times in life you achieve something and you think you really are something, but then that's the problem. People look after you all the time, people talk about you so you start to think that you are something, but you are nothing. Every time you achieve something you must understand that you still have higher things to achieve, and be humble and keep your feet on the floor.'

Basso's philosophy on success

PLAYERS OF THE YEAR

The list of City players winning the club's Player of the
Year Award since 1968 is as follows:

Season	Player
1967/68	John Quigley
1968/69	Bobby Kellard
1969/70	Dickie Rooks
1970/71	Bryan Drysdale
1971/72	Geoff Merrick
1972/73	John Emanuel
1973/74	Gerry Gow
1974/75	Gary Collier
1975/76	The Whole Team
1976/77	Norman Hunter
1977/78	Norman Hunter
1978/79	Gerry Gow
1979/80	Geoff Merrick
1980/81	Kevin Mabbutt
1981/82	Mick Harford
1982/83	Glyn Riley
1983/84	Howard Pritchard
1984/85	Alan Walsh
1985/86	Bobby Hutchison
1986/87	Rob Newman
1987/88	Alan Walsh
1988/89	Keith Waugh
1989/90	Bob Taylor
1990/91	Andy Llewellyn
1991/92	Martin Scott
1992/93	Keith Welch
1993/94	Wayne Allison
1994/95	Matt Bryant

1995/96	Martin Kuhl
1996/97	Shaun Taylor
1997/98	Shaun Taylor
1998/99	Ade Akinbiyi
1999/2000	Billy Mercer
2000/01	Brian Tinnion
2001/02	Matt Hill
2002/03	Scott Murray
2003/04	Tommy Doherty
2004/05	Leroy Lita
2005/06	Steve Brooker
2006/07	Jamie McCombe
2007/08	Adriano Basso
2008/09	Dele Adebola
2009/10	Cole Skuse
2010/11	Albert Adomah
2011/12	Jon Stead

CITY'S COMPLETE FA CUP RECORD

1897/98

R1	Clifton	H	9–1
	Wylllie, Carnelly (4), O'Brien (+3 goals uncredited)		
R2	Trowbridge	A	5–2
	Caie, Higgins (3), Carnelly		
R3	Southampton	A	0–2

1898/99

R1	Cowes	A	5–0
	Caie, O'Brien, Russell, Langham, Finnerham		
R2	Bristol St George	A	1–0
	Finnerham		

R3	Reading	H	3–2
	Langham, Caie (2)		
R4	Sunderland	H	2–4
	Langham, Finnerham		

1899/1900

R1	Stalybridge R	H	2–1
	Jones, Blessington		
R2	Aston Villa	A	1–5
	Jones		

1900/01

R1	Reading	A	1–1
	Fulton		
R1r	Reading	H	0–0
R1r2	Reading	N	1–2
	Michael (played at Swindon)		

1901/02

R1	Bristol East	H	5–1
	S. Jones, Cookson (2), W. Jones, og		
R2	Bristol Rovers	A	0–2A (fog)
R2	Bristol Rovers	A	1–1
	Bradbury		
R2r	Bristol Rovers	H	2–2
	Cookson, McLean		

1902/03

R1	Middlesbrough	H	3–1
	Wombwell, Boucher, Leigh		
R2	Bolton W	H	5–0
	Banks (3), Wombwell, Dean		
R3	Tottenham	A	0–1

1903/04

| R1 | New Brompton | A | 1–1 |
| | Wombwell | | |

R1r	New Brompton	H	5–2
	Hoise, Fisher, Corbett, Morris, og		
R2	Sheffield Utd	H	1–3
	Hoise		

1904/05

R1	Blackpool	H	2–1
	Jones, Gilligan		
R2	W Arsenal	A	0–0
R2r	W Arsenal	H	1–0
	Dean		
R3	Preston NE	H	0–0
R3r	Preston NE	A	0–1

1905/06

R1	Brentford	A	1–2
	Maxwell		

1906/07

R1	Leeds City	H	4–1
	Gilligan (2), Burton, Maxwell		
R2	W Arsenal	A	1–2
	Gilligan		

1907/08

R1	Grimsby Town	H	0–0
R1r	Grimsby Town	A	1–2
	Hilton		

1908/09

R1	Southampton	H	1–1
	Rippon		
R1r	Southampton	A	2–0
	Rippon (pen), Hardy		
R2	Bury		H 2–2
	Gilligan, Burton		

R2r	Bury	A	1–0
	Gilligan		
R3	Norwich City	H	2–0
	Burton, Rippon		
R4	Glossop NE	A	0–0
R4r	Glossop NE	H	1–0
	Gilligan		
S-F	Derby County	N	1–1
	Rippon (pen) (at Stamford Bridge)		
S-Fr	Derby County	N	2–1
	Rippon (pen), Hardy (at St Andrews)		
F	Manchester Utd	N	0–1
	(at The Crystal Palace)		

1909/10

R1	Liverpool	H	2–0
	Rippon, Burton		
R2	West Brom	H	1–1
	Gilligan		
R2r	West Brom	A	2–4
	Staniforth, Gilligan		

1910/11

| R1 | Crewe A | H | 0–3 |

1911/12

| R1 | Liverpool | A | 0–3 |

1912/13

| R1 | Northampton T | A | 0–1 |

1913/14

R1	QPR	A	2–2
	Picken, Brown		
R1r	QPR	H	0–2

1914/15

| R1 | Cardiff City | H | 2–0 |
| | Burton (2) | | |

R2	Everton	A	0–4

1919/20

R1	Grimsby Town	A	2–1
	Howarth (2)		
R2	Arsenal	H	1–0
	Howarth		
R3	Cardiff City	H	2–1
	Howarth, Neesam		
R4	Bradford City	H	2–0
	Harris (2)		
S-F	Huddersfield T	N	1–2
	Howarth (at Stamford Bridge)		

1920/21

R1	Aston Villa	A	0–2

1921/22

R1	Nottingham F	H	0–0
R1r	Nottingham F	A	1–3
	Bown		

1922/23

R1	Wrexham	H	5–1
	Fairclough (3), Paul, Walker		
R2	Derby County	H	0–3

1923/24

R1	Norwich City	A	1–0
	Smailes		
R2	Sheffield W	A	1–1
	Pocock		
R2r	Sheffield W	H	2–0
	Walsh (2)		
R3	Cardiff City	A	0–3

1924/25

R1	Bristol Rovers	A	1–0
	Walsh		

| R2 | Liverpool | A | 0–1 |

1925/26

| R1 | West Brom | A | 1–4 |
| | Pocock | | |

1926/27

R1	Merthyr Town	A	2–0
	Foster, Paul		
R2	Bournemouth	H	1–1
	Martin		
R2r	Bournemouth	A	0–2

1927/28

| R1 | Tottenham | H | 1–2 |
| | Martin | | |

1928/29

| R1 | Liverpool | H | 0–2 |

1929/30

| R1 | Derby County | A | 1–5 |
| | Williams | | |

1930/31

| R1 | Barnsley | A | 1–4 |
| | Vials | | |

1931/32

R1	Notts County	A	2–2
	Elliot (2)		
R1r	Notts County	H	3–2
	Williams (2), Elliot		
R2	Watford	A	1–2
	Elliot		

1932/33

| R1 | Romford | H | 4–0 |
| | Bowen (3), Loftus | | |

R2	Tranmere R	H	2–2
	Keating, Loftus		
R2r	Tranmere R	A	2–3
	Loftus, Bowen		

1933/34

R1	Kingstonians	A	7–1
	Brinton (2), Heale (2), Reed (2), Riley		
R2	Barrow	H	2–1
	Riley, Cainey		
R3	Derby County	H	1–1
	Scriven		
R3r	Derby County	A	0–1

1934/35

R1	Gillingham	H	2–0
	Landells (2)		
R2	Rotherham	A	2–1
	Loftus (2)		
R3	Bury	H	1–1
	Harston		
R3r	Bury	A	2–2
	Hodge, Harston		
R3r2	Bury	N	2–1
	Hodge (2) (at Villa Park)		
R4	Portsmouth	A	0–0
R4r	Portsmouth	H	2–0
	Hodge, Harston		
R5	Preston NE	H	0–0
R5r	Preston NE	A	0–5

1935/36

| R1 | Crystal Palace | H | 0–1 |

1936/37

| R1 | Newport County | A | 0–3 |

1937/38

R1	Enfield	H	3–0

Haycock (2), og

R2	Cardiff City	A	1–1

Brain

R2r	Cardiff City	H	0–2

1945/46

R1 (1)	Yeovil & Petters	A	2–2

Artus, Curran

R1 (2)	Yeovil & Petters	H	3–0

Curran, Chilcott, Clark

R2 (1)	Bristol Rovers	H	4–2

Morgan (2), Williams (2)

R2 (2)	Bristol Rovers	A	2–0

Chilcott, Clark

R3 (1)	Swansea Town	H	5–1

Clark (3), Bentley, Chilcott

R3(2)	Swansea Town	A	2–2

Williams, Chilcott

R4 (1)	Brentford	H	2–1

Hargreaves, Williams

R4 (2)	Brentford	A	0–5

1946/47

R1	Hayes	H	9–3

Clark (5), Chilcott, Williams (2), Hargreaves

R2	Gillingham	H	1–2

Clark

1947/48

R1	Dartford	A	0–0
R1r	Dartford	H	9–2

Townsend (3), Clark (3), Williams (3)

R2	Crystal Palace	H	0–1

1948/49

R1	Crystal Palace	H	1–0

Townsend

R2	Swansea Town	H	3–1

Boxshall, Townsend, Barney

R3	Chelsea	H	1–3

Clark

1949/50

R1	Nottingham F	A	0–1

1950/51

R1	Gloucester City	H	4–0

Guy, Peacock, Rodgers, Rogers

R2	Wrexham	H	2–1

Williams, Rogers

R3	Blackburn R	H	2–1

Rodgers (2)

R4	Brighton	H	1–0

Clark

R5	Birmingham C	A	0–1

1951/52

R1	Brighton	A	2–1

Atyeo (2)

R2	Colchester	A	1–2

Masters

1952/53

R1	Coventry City	A	0–2

1953/54

R1	Torquay Utd	A	3–1

Atyeo, Micklewright (2)

R2	Rhyl	A	3–0

Micklewright, Atyeo, Williams

R3	Rotherham	H	1–3

Atyeo

1954/55

R1	Southend Utd	H	1–2

Rodgers

1955/56

R1	Everton	A	1–3

Atyeo

1956/57

R1	Rotherham	H	4–1

Curtis, Atyeo (2), Hinshelwood

R2	Rhyl	H	3–0

Etheridge, Atyeo (2)

R3	Aston Villa	A	1–2

Atyeo

1957/58

R1	Accrington S	A	2–2

Hinshelwood, Curtis

R1r	Accrington S	H	3–1

Atyeo (2), Curtis

R2	Notts County	A	2–1

Etheridge, Hinshelwood

R3	Bristol Rovers	H	3–4

Watkins, Etheridge, Burden

1958/59

R1	Doncaster R	A	2–0

Tindill, Watkins

R2	Blackpool	H	1–1

Tindill

R2r	Blackpool	A	0–1

1959/60

R1	Charlton Ath	H	2–3

Atyeo, Cavanagh

1960/61

R1	Chichester	H	11–0

Atyeo (5), A Williams (3), Tait, R Williams, Bailey (og)

R2	King's Lynn	A	2–2

Atyeo, Rogers

R2r	King's Lynn	H	3–0

Atyeo, Rogers (2)

R3	Plymouth	A	1–0

R Williams

R4A	Leicester C	A	0–0

Abandoned due to waterlogged pitch

R4	Leicester C	A	1–5

og

1961/62

R1	Hereford Utd	H	1–1

Tait

R1r	Hereford Utd	A	5–2

Atyeo (2), Williams, Tait, Etheridge

R2	Dartford	H	8–2

Tait (3), Derrick (2), Atyeo, Connor, Rogers

R3	Walsall	H	0–0
R3r	Walsall	A	1–4

Derrick

1962/63

R1	Wellington	H	4–2

Etheridge (pen), Atyeo (2), Derrick

R2	Wimbledon	H	2–1

Clark (2)

R3	Aston Villa	H	1–1

Clark

R3r	Aston Villa	A	2–3

Williams, Etheridge

1963/64

R1	Corby Town	A	3–1
	Low, Clark, Williams		
R2	Exeter City	A	2–0
	(no record of scorers)		
R3	Doncaster R	A	2–2
	(no record of scorers)		
R3r	Doncaster R	H	2–0
	(no record of scorers)		
R4	Sunderland	A	1–6

1964/65

R1	Brighton	H	1–0
	Savino		
R2	Bournemouth	A	3–0
	Clark, Sharp (2)		
R3	Sheffield Utd	H	1–1
	Ford (pen)		
R3r	Sheffield Utd	A	0–3

1965/66

R3	Birmingham C	A	2–3
	Bush, Low		

1966/67

R3	Halifax Town	A	1–1
	Peters		
R3r	Halifax Town	H	4–1
	Crowe (2), Peters, Down		
R4	Southampton	H	1–0
	Bush		
R5	Tottenham	A	0–2

1967/68

R3	Bristol Rovers	H	0–0
R3r	Bristol Rovers	A	2–1
	Crowe, Galley		

R4	Middlesbrough	A	1–1
	Garland		
R4r	Middlesbrough	H	2–1
	Connor, Galley		
R5	Leeds Utd	A	0–2

1968/69

| R3 | West Ham | A | 2–3 |
| | Galley, Skirton | | |

1969/70

| R3 | Chester | A | 1–2 |
| | Skirton | | |

1970/71

| R3 | Southampton | A | 0–3 |

1971/72

| R3 | Preston NE | A | 2–4 |
| | Spiring, Wilson | | |

1972/73

R3	Portsmouth	A	1–1
	Gould		
R3r	Portsmouth	H	4–1
	Gould, Tainton, Sweeney, Gow (pen)		
R4	Wolves	A	0–1

1973/74

R3	Hull City	H	1–1
	Merrick		
R3r	Hull City	A	1–0
	Tainton		
R4	Hereford Utd	A	1–0
	Merrick		
R5	Leeds United	H	1–1
	Fear		
R5r	Leeds United	A	1–0
	Gillies		
R6	Liverpool	H	0–1

1974/75

R3	Sheffield Utd	A	0–2

1975/76

R3   Coventry City   A   1–2
      Brolly

1976/77

R3   Ipswich Town   A   1–4
      Fear

1977/78

R3   Wrexham   H   4–4
      Mabbutt (2), Ritchie, Cormack
R3   Wrexham   A   0–3

1978/79

R3   Bolton W   H   3–1
      Gow, Rodgers, Ritchie
R4   Crystal Palace A   0–3

1979/80

R3   Derby County   H   6–2
      Garland (2), Pritchard (2), Whitehead, Mann
R4   Ipswich Town   H   1–2
      Whitehead

1980/81

R3   Derby County   A   0–0
R3r   Derby County   H   2–0
      Mabbutt, Ritchie
R4   Carlisle   A   1–1
      Mabbutt
R4r   Carlisle   H   5–0
      Mabbutt (2), Ritchie (2, 1pen), Mann
R5   Nottingham F   A   1–2
      Mabbutt

1981/82

R1	Torquay Utd	H	0–0
R1r	Torquay Utd	A	2–1
	Mann (2)		
R2	Northampton T	H	3–0
	Tainton, Harford (2)		
R3	Peterborough Utd	A	1–0
	Chandler		
R4	Aston Villa	H	0–1

1982/83

| R1 | Orient | A | 1–4 |
| | Johnson | | |

1983/84

R1	Corinthian CAS	A	0–0
	(played at Dulwich Hamlet)		
R1r	Corinthian CAS	H	4–0
	Riley, Pritchard (3)		
R2	Bristol Rovers	A	2–1
	Ritchie, Hirst		
R3	Notts County	A	2–2
	Crawford, Ritchie		
R3r	Notts County	H	0–2

1984/85

R1	Fisher Ath	A	1–0
	Riley		
R2	Bristol Rovers	H	1–3
	Halliday		

1985/86

R1	Swindon Town	A	0–0
R1r	Swindon Town	H	4–2
	Neville (3), Riley		
R2	Exeter City	H	1–2
	Walsh (pen)		

1986/87

R1	VS Rugby	H	3–1
	Marshall, Hutchison, Walsh		
R2	Bath City	H	1–1
	Neville		
R2r	Bath City	A	3–0
	Owen (2, 1pen), Neville (at Ashton Gate)		
R3	Plymouth	H	1–1
	Riley		
R3r	Plymouth	A	1–3
	Marshall		

1987/88

R1	Aylesbury Utd	H	1–0
	Caldwell		
R2	Torquay	H	0–1

1988/89

R1	Southend Utd	H	3–1
	Walsh, McGarvey, Shutt		
R2	Aldershot	A	1–1
	Shutt		
R2r	Aldershot	H	0–0
R2r2	Aldershot	A	2–2
	Shutt, Newman (pen)		
R2r3	Aldershot	H	1–0
	Shutt		
R3	Hartlepool	A	0–1

1989/90

R1	Barnet	H	2–0
	Taylor, Turner		
R2	Fulham	H	2–1
	Taylor, Wimbleton		
R3	Swindon Town	H	2–1
	Taylor, Newman		

R4	Chelsea	H	3–1
	Turner (2), Gavin		
R5	Cambridge U	H	0–0
R5r	Cambridge U	A	1–1
	Taylor		
R5r2	Cambridge U	A	1–5
	Taylor		

1990/91

R3	Norwich City	A	1–2
	Allison		

1991/92

R3	Wimbledon	H	1–1
	og		
R3r	Wimbledon	A	1–0
	May		
R4	Leicester City	A	2–1
	Bent, Dziekanowski		
R5	Nottingham F	A	1–4
	Dziekanowski		

1992/93

R3	Luton Town	A	0–2

1993/94

R3	Liverpool	H	1–1A
	Allison (abandoned due to floodlight failure)		
R3	Liverpool	H	1–1
	Allison		
R3r	Liverpool	A	1–0
	Tinnion		
R4	Stockport Co	A	4–0
	Shail, Allison (3)		
R5	Charlton Ath	H	1–1
	Tinnion		
R5r	Charlton Ath	A	0–2

1994/95

R3	Stoke City	H	0–0
R3r	Stoke City	A	3–1

Bent, Baird, Tinnion

R4	Everton	H	0–1

1995/96

R1	Bournemouth	A	0–0
R1r	Bournemouth	H	0–1

1996/97

R1	Swansea City	A	1–1

Kuhl

R1r	Swansea City	H	1–0

Agostino

R2	St Albans	H	9–2

Goodridge, Agostino (4), Kuhl, Hewlett (2), Nugent

R3	Chesterfield	A	0–2

1997/98

R1	Millwall	H	1–0

Taylor

R2	Bournemouth	A	1–3

Cramb

1998/99

R3	Everton	H	0–2

1999/2000

R1	Mansfield	H	3–2

Tinnion (2), Murray

R2	Bournemouth	A	2–0

Murray (2)

R3	Sheffield Wed	A	0–1

2000/01

R1	Chesterfield	A	1–0

Thorpe

R2	Kettering	H	3–1
	Peacock, Clist, Thorpe		
R3	Huddersfield T	A	2–0
	Clist, Beadle		
R4	Kingstonian	H	1–1
	Thorpe		
R4r	Kingstonian	A	1–0
	Thorpe		
R5	Leicester City	A	0–3

2001/02

R1	Orient	H	0–1

2002/03

R1	Heybridge Swifts	A	7–0
	Roberts (2), Tinnion (pen), Murray (2), Lita (2)		
R2	Harrogate R'way	A	3–1
	og, Murray, Roberts		
R3	Leicester City	A	0–2

2003/04

R1	Bradford City	A	5–2
Amankwaah (2), og, Wilkshire, Matthews			
R2	Barnsley	H	0–0
R2r	Barnsley	A	1–2
	Roberts		

2004/05

R1	Brentford	H	1–1
	Lita		
R1r	Brentford	A	1–1*
	Heffernan (*City lost 4–3 on pens)		

2005/06

R1	Notts County	H	0–2

2006/07

R1	York City	A	1–0

McCombe

R2	Gillingham	H	4–3

Jevons (3), Showunmi

R3	Coventry City	H	3–3

Brooker, Showunmi, Jevons

R3r	Coventry City	A	2–0

Murray, Showunmi

R4	Middlesbrough	H	2–2

Keogh, Murray

R4r	Middlesbrough	A	2–2*

Noble, McCombe (*City lost 5–4 on pens)

2007/08

R3	Middlesbrough	H	1–2

Fontaine

2008/09

R3	Portsmouth	A	0–0
R3r	Portsmouth	H	0–2

2009/10

R3	Cardiff City	H	1–1
R3r	Cardiff City	A	0–1

2010/11

R3	Sheffield Wed	H	0–3

2011/12

R3	Crawley	A	0–1

CITY'S COMPLETE LEAGUE CUP RECORD

Season	Opponent	Result	Round	H/A	Att
1960/61	Aldershot	1–1	LC–2	A	5,700
1960/61	Aldershot	3–0	LC–2R	H	9,229
1960/61	Nottingham F	1–2	LC–3	A	3,690
1961/62	York City	0–3	LC–1	A	8,379
1962/63	Rotherham Utd	1–2	LC–2	H	7,469
1963/64	Gillingham	2–4	LC–1	A	5,940
1964/65	Carlisle Utd	1–4	LC–2	A	10,055
1965/66	Shrewsbury T	0–1	LC–2	A	7,158
1966/67	Swansea Town	1–1	LC–2	H	6,952
1966/67	Swansea Town	1–2	LC–2R	A	5,466
1967/68	Everton	0–5	LC–2	H	22,054
1968/69	Newport C	2–0	LC–1	H	9,778
1968/69	Middlesbrough	1–0	LC–2	H	14,218
1968/69	Leeds Utd	1–2	LC–3	A	16,359
1969/70	Exeter City	1–1	LC–1	A	8,003
1969/70	Exeter City	3–2	LC–1R	H	10,915
1969/70	Leicester City	0–0	LC–2	H	15,883
1969/70	Leicester City	0–0	LC–2R	A	20,797
1969/70	Leicester City	1–3	LC–2R	A	12,600
1970/71	Rotherham Utd	0–0	LC–2	A	6,384
1970/71	Rotherham Utd	4–0	LC–2R	H	9,403
1970/71	Blackpool	1–0	LC–3	A	10,877
1970/71	Leicester City	2–2	LC–4	A	21,577
1970/71	Leicester City	2–1	LC–4R	H	16,575
1970/71	Fulham	0–0	LC–5	A	16,281
1970/71	Fulham	1–0	LC–5R	H	23,228
1970/71	Tottenham H	1–1	LC–SF (1)	H	30,022
1970/71	Tottenham H	0–2	LC–SF (2)	A	29,982
1971/72	Plymouth A	0–1	LC–1	A	11,248
1972/73	West Ham Utd	1–2	LC–2	A	17,688
1973/74	Scunthorpe Utd	0–0	LC–2	A	4,418
1973/74	Scunthorpe Utd	2–1	LC–2R	H	7,837
1973/74	Coventry City	2–2	LC–3	H	19,129
1973/74	Coventry City	1–2	LC–3R	A	13,049

1974/75	Cardiff City	2–1	LC–1	H	8,813
1974/75	Crystal Palace	4–1	LC–2	A	16,263
1974/75	Liverpool	0–0	LC–3	H	25,573
1974/75	Liverpool	0–4	LC–3R	A	23,694
1975/76	West Ham Utd	0–0	LC–2	A	19,837
1975/76	West Ham Utd	1–3	LC–2R	H	19,643
1976/77	Coventry City	0–1	LC–2	H	13,878
1977/78	Stoke City	1–0	LC–2	H	11,877
1977/78	Wrexham	0–1	LC–3	A	10,183
1978/79	Crystal Palace	1–2	LC–2	H	10,433
1979/80	Rotherham Utd	1–0	LC–2 (1)	H	6,981
1979/80	Rotherham Utd	1–1	LC–2 (2)	A	7,327
1979/80	Peterborough Utd	1–1	LC–3	A	7,067
1979/80	Peterborough Utd	4–0	LC–3R	H	9,125
1979/80	Nottingham F	1–1	LC–4	H	25,695
1979/80	Nottingham F	0–3	LC–4R	A	20,462
1980/81	Birmingham C	1–2	LC–2 (1)	A	12,163
1980/81	Birmingham C	0–0	LC–2 (2)	H	6,958
1981/82	Walsall	2–0	LC–1 (1)	H	3,906
1981/82	Walsall	0–1	LC–1 (2)	A	2,830
1981/82	Carlisle United	0–0	LC–2 (1)	A	4,111
1981/82	Carlisle United	2–1	LC–2 (2)	H	5,220
1981/82	QPR	0–3	LC–3	A	9,215

Milk Cup

1982/83	Swindon Town	1–2	LC–1/1	A	3,736
1982/83	Swindon Town	2–0	LC–1/2	H	3,786
1982/83	Sheffield Wed	1–2	LC–2/1	H	4,486
1982/83	Sheffield Wed	1–1	LC–2/2	A	7,920
1983/84	Oxford Utd	1–1	LC–1/1	A	3,924
1983/84	Oxford Utd	0–1	LC–1/2	H	5,233
1984/85	Newport C	2–1	LC–1/1	H	5,424
1984/85	Newport C	3–0	LC–1/2	A	3,276
1984/85	West Ham Utd	2–2	LC–2/1	H	15,894
1984/85	West Ham Utd	1–6	LC–2/2	A	11,376
1985/86	Hereford Utd	1–5	LC–1/1	A	2,449
1985/86	Hereford Utd	2–0	LC–1/2	H	2,373

Littlewoods Cup

1986/87	Bournemouth	1–0	LC–1/1	A	2,631
1986/87	Bournemouth	1–1	LC–1/2	H	4,776
1986/87	Sheffield Utd	2–2	LC–2/1	H	8,366
1986/87	Sheffield Utd	0–3	LC–2/2	A	5,587
1987/88	Swindon Town	0–3	LC–1/1	A	6,807
1987/88	Swindon Town	3–2	LC–1/2	H	7,013
1988/89	Exeter City	1–0	LC–1/1	H	6,005
1988/89	Exeter City	1–0	LC–1/2	A	2,749
1988/89	Oxford United	4–2	LC–2/1	A	3,705
1988/89	Oxford United	2–0	LC–2/2	H	6,255
1988/89	Crystal Palace	4–1	LC–3	H	12,167
1988/89	Tranmere R	1–0	LC–4	H	11,110
1988/89	Bradford City	1–0	LC–5	A	15,330
1988/89	Nottingham F	1–1	LC–SF/1	A	30,016
1988/89	Nottingham F	0–1	LC–SF/2	H	28,084
1989/90	Reading	2–3	LC–1/1	H	6,318
1989/90	Reading	2–2	LC–1/2	A	4,457

Rumbelows Cup

1990/91	West Brom	2–2	LC–1/1	A	8,721
1990/91	West Brom	1–0	LC–1/2	H	9,851
1990/91	Sunderland	1–0	LC–2/1	A	10,358
1990/91	Sunderland	1–6	LC–2/2	H	11,776
1991/92	Bristol Rovers	3–1	LC–2/1	A	5,155
1991/92	Bristol Rovers	2–4	LC–2/2	H	9,880

Coca-Cola Cup

1992/93	Cardiff City	0–1	LC–1/1	A	7,708
1992/93	Cardiff City	5–1	LC–1/2	H	9,801
1992/93	Sheffield United	2–1	LC–2/1	H	6,922
1992/93	Sheffield United	1–4	LC–2/2	A	7,588
1993/94	Swansea City	1–0	LC–1/1	A	3,746
1993/94	Swansea City	0–2	LC–1/2	H	4,633
1994/95	Notts County	0–1	LC–2/1	H	2,546
1994/95	Notts County	0–3	LC–2/2	A	2,271
1995/96	Colchester Utd	1–2	LC–1/1	A	2,831
1995/96	Colchester Utd	2–1	LC–1/2	H	3,684
1995/96	Newcastle Utd	0–5	LC–2/1	H	15,952
1995/96	Newcastle Utd	1–3	LC–2/2	A	36,357

1996/97	Torquay Utd	3–3	LC–1/1	A	2,824
1996/97	Torquay Utd	1–0	LC–1/2	H	4,513
1996/97	Bolton W	0–0	LC–2/1	H	6,351
1996/97	Bolton W	1–3	LC–2/2	A	6,367
1997/98	Bristol Rovers	0–0	LC–1/1	H	9,341
1997/98	Bristol Rovers	2–1	LC–1/2	A	5,872
1997/98	Leeds United	1–3	LC–2/1	A	8,806
1997/98	Leeds United	2–1	LC–2/2	H	10,857
1998/99	Shrewsbury T	4–0	LC–1/1	H	3,585
1998/99	Shrewsbury T	3–4	LC–1/2	A	1,011
1998/99	Crewe A	1–1	LC–2/1	H	3,082
1998/99	Crewe A	0–2	LC–2/2	A	3,089

Worthington Cup

1999/00	Cambridge Utd	2–2	LC–1/1	A	2,813
1999/00	Cambridge Utd	2–1	LC–1/2	H	5,352
1999/00	Nottingham F	1–2	LC–2/1	A	5,015
1999/00	Nottingham F	0–0	LC–2/2	H	8,259
2000/01	Brentford	2–2	LC–1/1	H	3,471
2000/01	Brentford	1–2	LC–1/2	A	2,310
2001/02	Cheltenham T	2–1	LC–1	H	5,367
2001/02	Watford	2–3	LC–2	H	7,256
2002/03	Oxford Utd	0–1	LC–1	H	4,065

Carling Cup

2003/04	Swansea City	4–1	LC–1	H	5,870
2003/04	Watford	1–0	LC–2	H	5,213
2003/04	Southampton	0–3	LC–3	H	17,408
2004/05	Wycombe W	1–0	LC–1	A	1,778
2004/05	Everton	2–2	LC–2	H	15,264
2005/06	Barnet	2–4	LC–1	H	3,383
2006/07	Cheltenham T	1–2	LC–1	A	3,713
2007/08	Brentford	3–0	LC–1	A	2,213
2007/08	Man City	1–2	LC–2	H	14,541
2008/09	Peterborough Utd	2–1	LC–1	H	5,684
2008/09	Crewe A	1–2	LC–2	A	3,227
2009/10	Brentford	1–0	LC-1	A	3,024
2009/10	Carlisle	0–2	LC-2	H	6,359
2010/11	Southend	3–2	LC-1	A	2,940
2011/12	Swindon	0–1	LC-1	H	7,708